SUSY
ATKINS

# THE REALLY USEFUL GUIDE TO RED WINE.

EDITORIAL DIRECTOR Jane O'Shea
CREATIVE DIRECTOR Helen Lewis
PROJECT EDITOR Lisa Pendreigh
EDITOR Laura Herring
DESIGNER Claire Peters
PHOTOGRAPHER William Reavell
PRODUCTION Funsho Asemota

First published in 2006 by
Quadrille Publishing Ltd
Alhambra House
27–31 Charing Cross Road
London WC2H 0LS
www.quadrille.co.uk

Cataloguing in Publication Data: a catalogue
record for this book is available from the
British Library.

ISBN-13: 978 1 84400 290 0
ISBN-10: 1 84400 290 X
Printed in China

# THE REALLY USEFUL
# GUIDE TO RED WINE

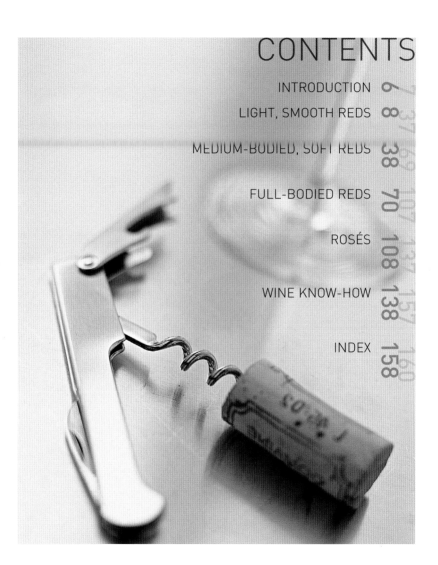

# CONTENTS

NEVER BEFORE HAVE SO MANY PEOPLE WANTED TO LEARN ABOUT WINE. Red wine in particular became hugely popular in the 1990s, when the health benefits of drinking moderate amounts were widely publicised. Combined with a distinct improvement in the quality of cheaper bottles, this meant huge numbers were converted to the pleasures of a glass of red.

Red wine can seem a hugely difficult subject. In particular, the great classic wines, such as claret (red Bordeaux), Burgundy, Tuscan reds and Spanish Rioja, are often intimidating to the beginner, who simply wants a key to getting great flavours at good value. This book aims to demystify the subject, presenting the facts at a glance in a way that should inspire everyone discovering a love for wine. You'll find plenty on those classics, as well as the popular modern reds from Australia, California, Chile and so on.

The book is arranged in terms of style – light, smooth reds; medium-bodied, soft reds; full-bodied reds and rosés. This helps you identify the bottles that suit you best – or, rather, which suit certain occasions or particular dishes. Talking of dishes, most red wines are meant to be enjoyed with food, so there are hints throughout on food and wine matches, and tips on how to buy, store and serve your reds so you get the very best out of them.

You'll notice a few recommended labels or wineries throughout the book. These are names I rate, but be aware it is nowhere near a comprehensive list and indeed in some larger regions I have sometimes avoided specific recommendations – there simply wasn't room. In short, where there are recommendations, these make good starting points, but there are plenty more great wines to discover!

# LIGHT, SMOOTH REDS

**8**
37

THE MOST FAMOUS LIGHT RED OF ALL IS BEAUJOLAIS. This is a wine which at best is joyfully summery, scented and fruity, packed with soft, tangy strawberries, but which all too often tastes tart and characterless. Bad Beaujolais is a serious turn-off, especially in these days of reliable, juicy, warm-climate wines. Recently it seems heavyweight wines have swept us off our feet – think Châteauneuf-du-Pape or California Cabernet – with the unfortunate result that some delightfully seductive and subtle reds have become overlooked. Don't make this mistake. There are certain key wine-drinking moments when a light and/or smooth red is the better choice by far, just so long as you select wisely.

For example, do you really want a blockbuster Aussie Shiraz or spicy, full-on Rhône red when you're sitting outside in hot weather, eating delicate summer dishes? I didn't think so. This is decidedly the occasion for a more restrained smoothie like Pinot Noir or a cool-climate Cabernet Franc. If your palate is fatigued from ultra-ripe fruit and heavy tannins, they are exactly what you should turn to. Don't be afraid to chill these wines a little, either; a touch of cold emphasises their fresh, cherry-berry succulence.

Strictly speaking, not all the wines discussed here are 'light'. Pinot Noir gives an impression of being light. But it can also be concentrated in its fruitiness, with beguiling, intense layers of chocolate, nuts and even cream. So 'smooth' is the adjective that applies here, rather than light. Gamay, the Beaujolais grape, often produces trite, weakling wines, like Beaujolais Nouveau, but the finest Beaujolais *crus* ('growths') have an admirable depth of flavour, plushy and lingering, rather than tough and tannic. So think refreshing and mellow in the case of the most tempting wines that follow. Not necessarily featherweight, but with a certain lightness of touch.

## APPEARANCE

Less concentrated and densely coloured than the rich, tannic reds. Expect a bright red-garnet colour, not the black-purple intensity of heftier wines. Very young bottles might have a bluish tinge; older ones are more brick-coloured.

## TEXTURE

Think soft and juicy, silky and mellow, without the heavy tannins of richer reds. The lightest, leanest wines taste insubstantial, jammy, even thin, while a fine Burgundy should be velvet-smooth, ripe and rounded.

## AROMA

A high-summer perfume of fresh red berries is often found, especially strawberries, although sniff for raspberries, red cherries, cranberries and plums, too. Loire reds have a leafy character and perhaps a hint of green capsicum. Beaujolais can have an estery aroma of pear-drops or banana chews; underripe wines sometimes smell of green beans and mown grass.

## FLAVOUR

Those red-berry fruits again, fresh and squishily ripe. There are sometimes hints of earth, game and spice in older burgundies, some say even stables and horse manure! Look out for layers of chocolate, coffee and toasted nuts.

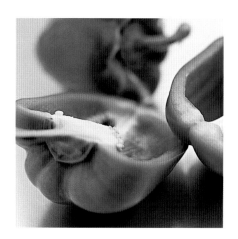

# PINOT NOIR

## SMOOTH, SILKY AND SOFT AS CRUSHED VELVET

It's not always light by any means, but Pinot Noir is (or should be) wonderfully smooth, silky and soft as crushed velvet. This is one of the greatest red grapes in the world, producing wines with a lovely, lush strawberry perfume and flavour when young, which matures into more farmyardy, gamey depths.

It is also one of the most difficult vines, requiring much tender, loving care and sensitivity in the vineyard and winery unless it is to go horribly wrong and produce an insipid, jammy stew. So for many ambitious winemakers, Pinot Noir is the holy grail – they are determined to master such a pernickety variety and make a show-stopping red from it.

So how do they make great Pinot Noir? This is a thin-skinned grape which succumbs easily to rot and disease, so the right conditions are crucial. It needs the correct soils (limestone is a plus), reasonably dry conditions (dampness is a minus) and the grape-growers must watch their yields very carefully, keeping them low if they want to avoid producing a wine that is too dilute.

Although winemakers across the globe strive hard to get it right, the best wines arguably still come from the Burgundy region in France, where winemakers have had centuries of experience with this notoriously temperamental vine. Plenty of basic (and not so basic)

Burgundy is poor, but the top wines are sublime. Other countries getting the better of this grape are the United States, New Zealand and Chile. If you've had a bad experience with Pinot Noir, don't just give up on it, as when this grape is good, it is really very good indeed, with a complexity, concentration and soft, sexy gorgeousness unrivalled by any of the other smooth, light reds. Just be sure to tread very carefully!

## FRANCE

Pinot Noir isn't found in vast numbers across French winemaking regions; instead it is concentrated in two or three. The most important, of course, is Burgundy. Put simply, white Burgundy is about Chardonnay, and red Burgundy is about Pinot Noir. Sure, a little wine is made from other red grapes in Burgundy, but Pinot Noir is what wine-lovers really want from this region: Pinot Noir that is sensual, perfumed and luscious, almost sweet with ripe fruitiness.

Sounds great, doesn't it? But here's a warning: to bag a truly super bottle and avoid the cheap, tart stuff, you need to know a bit about Burgundy and it is not an easy subject to get to grips with. Some Burgundy buffs devote their whole lives to unravelling the wines of this complex corner of France. This is partly because the area is split up into a patchwork of different small vineyards. Conscientious winemakers sweat to extract the individual character of each plot of land, imparting a sense of it in the finished wine. The French refer to this as *terroir* – the site, soil, sun, rainfall, slope – defining the quality and nature of the finished wine. It's the opposite of the large-scale southern-hemisphere, vine-growing region where an ocean of identical liquid flows from the same enormous tract of land. In Burgundy, Pinot Noir is crafted from minute nooks and crannies, and to understand it properly you need to get to know the area, its villages, its most important vineyards, and the characteristics of the individual wines made in them. In fact, to become a real Burgundy aficionado, you should visit the region and drive around, getting a feel of the land.

For those who want to appreciate red Burgundy from the comfort of their armchair, do be aware that the name of the place within the region, and even the specific vineyard site, is considered extremely important here. There are over one hundred appellations, ranging from generics like Bourgogne Rouge to the acclaimed *grands crus* that can be less than one hectare in size. Let's break them down into digestible nuggets of information: there are twenty-four sites designated *grands crus*, or 'best growths', for red wine, all in the Côte de Nuits except one: Corton. Then there are dozens of *premiers crus*, the next step down the ladder for top vineyard sites. All the *grand cru* and *premier cru* vineyards are named on the label. Blends of wines from *premier cru* sites are labelled 'premier cru' rather than with the name of an individual site, and then there are the wines that come from specific villages such as Givry or Chambolle-Musigny. Finally, at the bottom of the ladder, are the simple Bourgogne Rouge and the even more basic Bourgogne Grand Ordinaire.

Of course, the producers are important, although you would be forgiven for thinking that Burgundy was entirely about parcels of land, not winemakers. Some of the best Burgundian names to sample are Joseph Drouhin, Domaine Leroy, Louis Jadot and Domaine de la Romanée-Conti. Prices are certainly on the high side. It should be said that red Burgundy only becomes reliable if you ignore the bargain basement. In fact, it only becomes interesting and worthwhile once prices are steep. If all the above were not enough to put off the everyday tippler, this is a region of highly variable vintages, so pick wines from a fine year – 2001–04, 1999, 1996, 1995 rather than a rotten one!

Some Pinot Noir is also grown in the Loire Valley where it is notable for red Sancerre. There is another source of Pinot in France, and that's Alsace, in the eastern extremes of the country. This is a region renowned for white wines, with Pinot Noir its solitary red of any significance. The wines tend to be straightforward, fruity and light, with a wild strawberry perfume and flavour but little complexity. They are at their best served lightly chilled in the summer with fresh salmon: a rare partnership of red wine and fish.

## REST OF THE WORLD

Non-European winemakers struggle gamefully with Pinot Noir, usually looking to the magnificent wines of Burgundy as benchmarks and hoping to emulate them, or make a different but equally great version of their own. They don't always get it right by any means; a sweetish, red-berryish, lightish red of no distinction is more often the result, and frankly, that's a disappointment from such a potentially fascinating grape. Still, warmer-climate Pinot is gradually becoming better as grape-growers and winemakers are getting to grips with this quixotic vine.

Sometimes the wines from Oregon impress. The state was heralded as Pinot's 'second home' for a long time in the 1980s, then inconsistent quality and some poor vintages made critics think twice, but Oregon can still come up with the goods. Shame the wines are not cheaper, or more widely available.

California has some success with the grape if it is planted in areas such as Carneros, Russian River and Santa Barbara, where the hot sun is cooled by ocean breezes. Saintsbury, Au Bon Climat and Calera are producers to watch.

New Zealand has recently made a big splash with its Pinot Noir and certainly some fine examples have come out of the famous Marlborough region in the country's South Island. Indeed, it is good to see Pinot championed by the Kiwis, as other grapes, notably Cabernet, have trouble ripening in cooler climates. Pinot works better, as a recent flood of delicious new wines proves.

Other regions excelling with this grape are Martinborough on the North Island, and Central Otago, a dramatically beautiful area south of Marlborough, where there has been something of a 'gold rush' to plant vines lately. Central Otago's Pinots can be very impressive, with lots of concentration and ripe, smooth texture, but beware crazily high prices for some cult labels.

New Zealand's Pinot tends to be highly fruity, with an aromatic cherry-berry character. Look out for Isabel Estate, Martinborough Vineyards, Rippon and Mount Difficulty labels.

South Africa makes a handful of wines from Pinot that are more elegant and softer than its usual blockbuster reds. Find them from the Walker Bay/Hermanus coastal region. Chile can provide good-value, tasty Pinot, bursting with ripe red berry fruit and perhaps a note of smooth chocolate – recommended tasting. Back in Europe, Romania is a surprising source of decent Pinot Noir, especially from the Dealul Mare region, although these bottles are rarely seen on the shelves. And Germany makes palatable, light Pinot, most successfully in the Pfalz and Baden regions. Here the grape is called Spätburgunder.

# GAMAY (BEAUJOLAIS)

## LIGHT-HEARTED, EASY-GOING, MOREISH

It makes sense to deal with Gamay next, as it is the grape responsible for Beaujolais, and Beaujolais is made just south of Burgundy. For wine buffs, it will never rival Burgundy, but Beaujolais remains a much-loved red, and it can be wonderfully fruity, super-smooth and juicy, with the unmistakeable flavour of fresh red berries. Gamay has been described as the jester to king Pinot Noir: more light-hearted, easy-going, frivolous. Don't take Beaujolais too seriously, is the message, but don't dismiss it, either. It's one of the best reds to drink without food, as its moreish, succulent character means it slips down easily, and it makes a fine match for picnic fare – cold ham, sausage rolls, pâtés and quiches. Beaujolais may have fallen out of fashion since its seventies heyday, but it remains a crowd-pleaser.

That's the best possible picture of Beaujolais, anyway. The worst manifestation is dilute Beaujolais Nouveau, enjoyed more for the ritual of its arrival in the UK in November, soon after vintage, than the actual pleasure of its flavours. Poor Beaujolais (and there is plenty of it) has a smell like nail-varnish remover a sour-banana flavour and all the concentration of a classroom of ten-year-olds! Happily, there are some effective guidelines for avoiding the worst: side-step basic Beaujolais and Nouveau, and go for bottles labelled Beaujolais-Villages, wine made from grapes grown in better sites, or, best of all, those produced in ten named villages in the north of the region: Côte de Brouilly, Juliénas, Chiroubles, Moulin-à-Vent, Brouilly, St-Amour, Chénas, Fleurie, Morgon and Regnié. These have more depth of flavour, giving a much more satisfying glass of wine, with all the late-summer, squashily ripe, perfumed berry fruit you could possibly want. Georges Duboeuf (the best-known producer), is a good introduction, or try the wide range from Louis Jadot.

# CABERNET FRANC

## BEHIND THE LOIRE'S BEST REDS

Given the current trend for rich, powerful, ultra-fruity reds, it's not surprising that Cabernet Franc is relatively unknown. This is a shame, as the grape behind the Loire Valley's best reds offers wines with a fresh fragrance, plenty of raspberry character, and even a crunchy, pippy quality as if made from just-picked berries. You can almost smell the dew on the currant bushes here, perhaps catch a whiff of freshly mown grass. The best, though, have a ripe, concentrated core of red fruit (poor wines have an underripe, stalky nature). These are wines that seem to come from mid-, not late, summer, and should be served, perhaps lightly chilled, with a plate of ham salad or peppery cold beef.

Don't look for the grape variety on the label as you won't find it. Instead, find the location – Bourgeuil and Chinon offer the best examples. Try Pierre-Jacques Druet, Joguet, Domaine des Roches Neuves. Cabernet Franc is also grown in Bordeaux, where it's the third grape after Cabernet Sauvignon and Merlot in the claret blend, adding fragrance, in particular. Northern Italy also makes Cabernet Franc, but it's on the light, lean, slightly tart side – one for chilling lightly and quaffing on its own. In newer regions, winemakers have been slow to take up Cabernet Franc, except as a component in a blend, generally regarding it as a poor cousin to Cabernet Sauvignon. But one or two fine examples do exist, showing that fresh raspberry flavour.

# OTHER LIGHT, SMOOTH REDS

## PLENTY MORE TO PICK FROM

### LIGHT MERLOT

Merlot makes a range of styles, most of which are medium-bodied (see pages 46–53). Usually pretty smooth, fruity and soft, Merlot is the perfect blending partner for the more austere, tough Cabernet Sauvignon, in Bordeaux and elsewhere. On its own it ranges from lush, plummy, full, even oaky reds, to refreshingly light, almost grassy, wines. Northern Italy is the source of the most lean and elegant Merlot (or flavourless and insipid, depending on your producer and, to an extent, personal taste). In Bordeaux itself, cheaper reds have become generally a little more fruity and ripe-tasting of late, although some soft, simple, easy-drinking Merlot and Merlot-based bottles are available from the wider southwest area. Choose with care, though; inexpensive French Merlot can still be insipid.

### CORVINA

Not a well-known grape, but it is responsible, more than any other, for the popular Valpolicella of northeast Italy. 'Valpol' is a blend of grapes, but Corvina plays the biggest role, providing red-fruit flavour, and sometimes a hint of marzipan. Don't expect great things from basic Valpolicella, but enjoy the better examples, with their lively, youthful cherry fruit and reasonable depth of flavour.

## TARRANGO

The Tarrango grape gives Australia its very own take on Beaujolais: an extremely soft and easy-drinking red wine with the flavours of banana, cranberry and strawberry. It comes from an Australian cross between the Touriga and Sultana varieties, developed in the 1960s with the express purpose of providing a lighter red than usual in Australia. It needs plenty of heat and ripens well in Australia's warmer vineyards. Brown Brothers is the producer to look out for. Chill Tarrango well before serving and treat it as a simple but refreshing summer red.

## DORNFELDER

Not many people have heard of this grape, but it makes some tempting reds in Germany and even a few wines in England (think aromatic, tangy cherry and strawberry fruit, low tannins, easy to drink). Enjoy these wines when they are young, perhaps a little chilled.

## BONARDA

Argentinian softie, making very moreish (at best), very smooth, inexpensive reds that taste of squashy ripe cherries and cassis. Quality is a bit patchy and some wines are on the decidedly light side, but find a good, easy-drinking Bonarda and you have a good-value party red that all your guests should enjoy glugging with or without food. It's occasionally blended with other red grapes. Tesco's own-label Bonardas are a decent introduction.

## OTHER ITALIAN REDS

See pages 58–9, Dolcetto and Barbera, and be aware that sometimes these are made in a light, very soft style that could be placed in this category. There are several types of Italian red that count as light – Bardolino, for example, and Teroldego from the north-east. These can be juicy and moreish, at their best, but they are nevertheless fairly one-dimensional wines.

# MAKING THE DIFFERENCE

CARBONIC MACERATION IS THE TECHNICAL TERM FOR THE TRADITIONAL METHOD OF MAKING BEAUJOLAIS (see page 23). Instead of crushing the fruit, winemakers leave the bunches of grapes to ferment whole in vats, until they collapse and give up their juice. This results in a soft, juicy style of wine, as the tannins that are released from crushed skins, stalks and pips do not appear to such a great degree as they do in other red wines.

# MATCHING LIGHT, SMOOTH REDS WITH FOOD

LIGHT, SMOOTH REDS ARE A SENSIBLE CHOICE IF YOU WANT TO DRINK RED WINE ON ITS OWN, AS THEY ARE EASY TO ENJOY AND HAVE LESS TANNIN THAN OTHER TYPES OF RED. But these wines go well with food, too, as long as you don't overpower them. Heavy stews, roast lamb and chilli con carne are out; so instead match light reds like Beaujolais, Tarrango and Valpolicella with simple pasta dishes, pizzas and mild cheeses. They have an advantage with creamy sauces, as tannins often clash with cream. That said, fine Pinot Noir goes well with game birds or roast chicken, beef and duck. Choose an older wine with gamier meats. Try red Burgundy with rich, creamy and pungent cheeses, too. Very light Pinot, such as that from Alsace, matches fresh salmon well.

# STORING AND SERVING

MOST OF THE LIGHTER REDS NEED DRINKING UP WHILE THEY ARE STILL YOUNG, FRESH AND VIBRANT WITH AROMATIC RED-BERRY FRUIT. The richest, smoothest examples may be different, though the most serious Beaujolais (the *crus* described on page 23) will last a few years in bottle and, of course, fine red Burgundy is a great 'ager', turning gamey, pungent, even horsey in bottle as it is cellared, often for decades. Serve these bigger soft reds at room temperature, but the lighter ones very slightly chilled to bring out their succulent character.

# FIRST TASTE

■ For those who are unfamiliar with the lighter reds, be prepared for a different 'mouth-feel' from these wines. They are not heavy, thick or tannic. EXPECT A SMOOTH, SOFT TEXTURE AND A FRESH, TANGY FINISH.

■ Before serving, CHILL THESE WINES LIGHTLY to emphasise their succulence.

■ The AROMA IS ESPECIALLY IMPORTANT in these types of wine. It should be a fresh, berryish perfume, appealing and summery.

# BUYER'S GUIDE

■ Avoid the cheapest Burgundy as it is likely to be disappointingly thin and jammy. THIS IS ONE AREA WHERE THE PRICIER BOTTLES REALLY CAN BE WORTH IT. Not all are good, by any means, but most of the 'bargains' are downright poor!

■ Likewise, steer clear of basic Beaujolais and especially the gimmicky Beaujolais Nouveau. Better Beaujolais is not terrifically expensive. TRADE UP TO BOTTLES LABELLED BEAUJOLAIS-VILLAGES or, even better, the individual villages, such as Fleurie or Morgon.

■ Cabernet Franc is not especially fashionable, but do TRY THE GREAT LOIRE REDS FOR A REFRESHING YET SATISFYING GLASS OF QUALITY LIGHTER RED. Look for the appellations Chinon, Saumur-Champigny and Bourgeuil on the label.

# MOVING ON

■ Dolcetto tends to give a more serious, soft Italian red than Valpolicella. IF YOU LIKE ITALIAN FOOD AND WINE, DO TRY DOLCETTO FROM PIEDMONT together with a rich pasta bake.

■ Reds from Germany and England will only appeal to the most devoted fan. If you fall into this category, GIVE GERMAN AND ENGLISH REDS A WHIRL. Be prepared for some inconsistencies but the occasional fragrant gem.

■ Pinot Noir is the best smooth red variety, and IT PAYS TO SAMPLE PLENTY OF EXAMPLES FROM DIFFERENT AREAS, both within and outside Burgundy, to appreciate how this grape varies according to its site.

THESE ARE THE MOST VERSATILE REDS OF ALL: SOFT AND SMOOTH ENOUGH TO BE THOROUGHLY ENJOYABLE WHEN DRUNK ON THEIR OWN, YET WITH SUFFICIENT DEPTH AND CONCENTRATION TO STAND UP TO A WIDE RANGE OF SAVOURY DISHES. They clash with very little, can be cracked open on lots of occasions, and rarely offend anyone. The medium-bodied reds are much-loved and appreciated for their easy-going character and their consummate food-friendly quality. Have I made them sound a tad simple? If so, then let me set the record straight. They can be wonderful, beautifully made, perfectly balanced and highly sophisticated. It's just that the smooth reds are not difficult in any way; they are not richly tannic, not tartly crisp, and not packed with heavy wood and spice. They are easy to drink, and hurrah for that.

So it's hardly surprising that wines such as French Merlot, Chianti (made from Sangiovese) and Rioja (Tempranillo) have proved so enduringly popular. In fact, it's difficult to think of many who dislike such wines, so I'm perhaps preaching to the converted here! But even if you already know and appreciate the medium-bodied reds, there are plenty of tips that can help you both to enjoy them more and to spend your money wisely. They may be easy-going, but there are nonetheless better moments than others for choosing them, perfect dishes for matching with them, and a few bottles that are well worth avoiding. Read on…

## APPEARANCE

Bright and lively, often a vivid ruby-red. Not particularly dense or deep, nor pale and weedy-looking. Some wines are a bit richer and more concentrated in colour, edging towards a plummy, youthful, purple-blue hue.

## TEXTURE

Juicy and rounded, with a smooth, succulent finish. These wines should not be too powerful; any heavy oaky or spiky tannins will seem out of balance. Then again, they should have some structure and body filling them out. Look for perfect poise, a balance between ripe fruit and fresh acidity, with some tannin to firm things up.

## AROMA

Ripe red fruits galore – plums, strawberries, raspberries, cherries – like a rich summer pudding. Don't expect the dewily fresh, newly squeezed fruit juice of the light reds, however. The perfume of these wines should spell late summer berries, generously fleshy and fulsome. There may be some seductive hints of chocolate, truffles, fresh tobacco, herbs and tea-leaves, with cream and vanilla in oaky examples, more 'green' stalky notes in unripe ones.

## FLAVOUR

Strawberries and plums crop up a lot here, as do creamy, soft depths with hints of vanilla (Rioja) and chocolate (some Merlot). Don't expect the spiciness of the full-bodied reds, but there are some savoury hints – soy, earth, pepper – and perhaps a luxurious finish of creamy coffee which leaves you wanting more. Some of these reds, especially the Italian ones, also have quite pronounced, tangy acidity, too: a twist of sour cherry drops on the finish.

# MERLOT

BEAUTIFULLY SUPPLE, PLUMP AND LOVABLE

At one point, a few years ago, there was nothing more fashionable than Merlot. Or to be more specific: Pomerol from Bordeaux, which is mainly Merlot; California Merlot; and at a lower price point, Chilean Merlot. Look around a busy smart restaurant and you can be sure there will still be lots of diners plumping for wines made from this grape. They may not know much about it, but they know what's hip and happening, and to some people that still means Merlot. Twenty years ago, it would have been unthinkable. Merlot was considered Cabernet's poor cousin, an inferior blending partner in Bordeaux, and a workhorse grape, turning out less-than-thrilling bottles in other parts of the globe.

So what has happened since? Why has Merlot undergone the sort of image transformation that Travolta was looking for when he met Tarantino? In part, it's due to many drinkers associating moderate red wine drinking with good health. They are keen to glug on red, believing it is beneficial to their hearts (and there is evidence to back this up), but they don't want a tough, hefty wine like our big reds (see 'Full-bodied Reds' on pages 70–107), or a light, pale red with no guts.

Instead, they want plenty of ripe, juicy fruit – a real red, if you like – but one that tastes soft and easy when young, with few harsh tannins. And one that is widely available and grown all over the world. Merlot fits the bill. One television programme on the health benefits of red wine, broadcast in America a few years ago, is widely considered responsible for giving Merlot's popularity a massive boost. Then there's the fact that it tastes pretty darn delicious. Merlot has a thoroughly appealing personality. It may not 'wow' you like a glass of blockbuster Aussie Shiraz, but Merlot is beautifully supple, plump and lovable. It has a friendly, plummy flavour, a smooth, rounded texture. It's too complex to be described as 'simple', like, say, Gamay, but nevertheless it is an easy wine to enjoy. Winemakers adore it, too: it ripens better than Cabernet in cooler spots and although it can make dilute, bland wine if poorly treated and over-cropped, it often obliges with generously fruity reds.

## FRANCE

I've probably made Merlot sound too jolly and one-dimensional. Anyone coming to the majestic wines of St-Emilion and Pomerol in Bordeaux, where a high proportion of the blend is Merlot, would beg to disagree. These reds show Merlot at its most serious, concentrated and venerable. In fact, if anyone ever tells you that Merlot counts for little in Bordeaux compared to King Cabernet, then a) tell them it's more widely planted than Cabernet, and b) get them a glass of one of the finest Pomerols and make them drink their words.

Cabernet Sauvignon, Merlot's great blending partner, does indeed hold sway in the Médoc region of France, where its austere cassis and tannin character is fleshed out by the more lush and fruity Merlot component. But on the 'right bank' regions of the Libournais area, and especially its appellations of St-Emilion and Pomerol, Merlot contributes sixty to one hundred per cent of the blend. The rest is usually Cabernet Franc or Cabernet Sauvignon. These wines are softer, smoother, more velvety than Cabernet-heavy Médoc wines, and they are unusually rich, inky and intense in ripe fruit flavour and have an extra sheen of oak from new barrel-ageing to round them off and add complexity. They age well for decades, yet when young are more approachable than other Médoc reds.

The famous châteaux of Pomerol command extremely high prices for their wines. A few are clearly overpriced, the wine often bought by fashion victims. Even so, if you ever get the chance to try fine Pomerol from a good vintage, snatch it! Top estates include Pétrus, l'Eglise-Clinet, Gazin, Lafleur, Le Pin, l'Evangile and Trotanoy. It's trickier to pin down the exact character of St-Emilion as many small-scale winemakers work there, producing a range of styles. Some make such small quantities that they are described as *garagistes*, implying that they make their wine in the garage! Ideally, one would repair to this picturesque town and set to work tasting a number *in situ*. You could go for wine from one of the sixty named *crus classés* (classed growths), but don't expect them to be equally good, or if you're feeling wealthy make straight for the great *châteaux* names, Cheval Blanc, Ausone and Figeac, among others.

Merlot is grown all over southwest France and makes up a high proportion of the blend in cheaper reds. Although it is sometimes (and in the case of cheap claret, almost always) dilute and jammy, it can be reasonable value for money, if you pick carefully. Avoid basic Bordeaux Rouge or cheap claret at all costs. Instead seek out wines from the Côtes de Blaye, Côtes de Castillon, Côtes de Francs and Côtes de Bourg. I can't tell you exactly how much Merlot will be in the blend for each wine, but a youngish bottle that is relatively soft and easy-going, with juicy, red-berry character, is likely to contain a high proportion. The back label will sometimes let you know. If you're on a budget, try the wines of a wider area, such as Marmandais, Buzet, Duras and Bergerac, too, as they are made from Bordeaux varieties, often leaning heavily towards Merlot in the blend. Don't miss the *Vin de Pays d'Oc* Merlot from the deep south of France, either. It may not set the world on fire for depth and complexity, but it is usually modern, fruit-driven, gluggable stuff at decent prices.

# REST OF EUROPE

Northern Italy makes a lighter, more refreshing style of Merlot that really belongs in the previous section, 'Light, Smooth Reds' (see pages 8–37). A few quite different and much more serious wines are produced in central Italy, especially Tuscany, where Merlot is one of the grapes used for the much-admired 'Super-Tuscans': a newish breed made with international grapes as well as local ones. Expect quite chunky, oaky Merlot, or delicious blends with Cabernet or with local grape Sangiovese. Prices are high, and results can be a bit erratic, but sometimes the Super-Tuscans do shine, especially those from top wineries Avignonesi, Castello di Brolio, Castello di Fonterutoli and Ornellaia. A few intensely plummy, fairly weighty Merlots are being made in Sicily by progressive wineries; these are reliable, good-value wines in the non-European, fruit-driven style.

Spanish reds are mainly made from Tempranillo, but Cabernet has gradually crept into more and more bottles, and so, to a lesser degree, has Merlot. The Navarra region, a neighbour of Rioja in northwest Spain, has a progressive, modern wine industry, so it is not surprising to see Merlot pop up there. Navarran Merlots are appealingly ripe and well-balanced, and usually a little oaky. Try Castillo de Montjardin or Palacio de la Vega. Find Merlot in Penedés (another go-ahead, fashion-conscious region), Somontano, and even in the blend for one of Spain's most acclaimed reds, Vega Sicilia from the Ribera del Duero region.

In fact, Merlot is stretching its trendy tendrils into almost every winemaking country these days. Austria produces some decent, chunky Bordeaux blends, or mixes of Bordeaux grapes with its own varieties, although these bottles are a rare find abroad. Greece has a few

Merlot plantings, and Eastern Europe turns out some good-value bottles, although these have been rather trumped in recent years by non-European cheapies. Still, some Bulgarian Merlot impresses for its clean, bright fruit and decent oak. It's a shame that Bulgaria's wine industry isn't in better shape, as quality is currently unreliable. If you find a good one, congratulate yourself, as you've probably got a bargain. Domaine Boyar's Blueridge label is a fairly safe bet.

## REST OF THE WORLD

Californians have taken Merlot to their hearts – literally, they hope, as they sip the stuff and wait to live that bit longer – and there's plenty around from the West Coast. The worst can be too sweetly ripe, with unsubtle oak and a confected finish, but the best are superb. Concentrated, even chunky wines, packed with plum, cherry and rich chocolate, are made in Napa Valley,

and other areas. Blends of Bordeaux grapes can be serious, too, although someone coined the rather horrible name 'Meritage' to label them. There is some evidence that the Merlot craze is wearing off a bit as punters get fed up with the poor, cheap wines. There will always be Merlot mania to some degree on the West Coast, however – let's hope only the best wines survive any future backlash. Try Duckhorn, Beringer, Newton and Shafer wines. And give Washington State Merlot a whirl, too; it may not be too familiar, but can be bright and lively, as can Long Island's rare take on this grape.

Australia has surprisingly few Merlots, despite its reputation as a red-wine producer extraordinaire. The Aussies have preferred to concentrate on grapes which flourish in their very warm vineyards, hence loads of Cabernet and Shiraz, but less Merlot. More has appeared in the last year or two, and some are impressively fruity. In New Zealand, Merlot is extremely promising, particularly from the relatively warm Hawke's Bay region of the country. As the Kiwis get to grips more firmly with red wines, we can expect greater things from their Merlot. Waiheke Island, a hot spot out in Auckland Harbour, is another place excelling with reds, and Bordeaux-style blends in particular. Successful wineries include Esk Valley, Sileni, Goldwater and Stonyridge. South Africa is another country that is starting to prove it can shine with Merlot – in this case, some remarkably ripe, dark wines, particularly from Stellenbosch, Paarl and Malmesbury regions. Plaisir de Merle, De Toren, Spice Route and Warwick all make admirable Merlots or Merlot blends.

A few promising Merlots are emerging from Argentina, but for now the Argentinian Malbecs and Syrahs are more impressive. Which leaves us with Chile and some of the best-value reds in the world. Chilean Merlot is immediately likeable, its delicious fresh fruit rounded out by a richer chocolate/mocha, even smoky note. Don't expect anything like the sophistication of top Bordeaux. These are wines for everyday drinking – okay, perhaps for Saturday night quaffing! Think medium-bodied, medium price. They are very reliable and justly popular. Oddly, a proportion of Chilean 'Merlot' was recently found to be another grape entirely, Carmenère, which has become muddled up in the vineyards. Carmenère is now being labelled as such, and luckily turns out to make rather good red in its own right, with a slightly more pronounced savoury/earthy character. Try both and see if you can tell them apart. Some of the best Chilean Merlot/Merlot blends are made by Viña Carmen, Casa Lapostolle and Villard wineries.

# OTHER MEDIUM-BODIED, SOFT REDS

## PLENTY MORE TO PICK FROM

### SANGIOVESE

Sangiovese means 'blood of Jove', which doesn't sound especially tempting, somehow. Never mind; it's one of Italy's premium grapes and the mainstay of Tuscan reds, where it forms the base for the world-famous and perennially popular Chianti. There are other grapes that are used in the Chianti blend, but Sangiovese is the principal variety, while Brunello di Montalcino, another Tuscan classic, is made solely from it.

This vine ripens slowly, and that can cause problems, namely stalky green wine from grapes that haven't had enough sun. There used to be plenty of poor Chianti around displaying exactly such a fault, but thankfully the problem is more firmly under control these days. In fact, cast all memories of cheap seventies' raffia flasks from your mind! Today, Chianti, and particularly Chianti Classico, from the heart of the region, is pretty good stuff, aromatic with strawberries, tea-leaves and fresh cigars, and with that tangy twist of slightly sour cherries to give it a fresh lift and make it food-friendly.

The most exciting wines, though, are the riper, beefier, heartier Chiantis – still refreshing and smooth, but without a trace of

weediness. Blends with Merlot (the dynamic new breed of 'Super-Tuscan' reds, see page 50) are interesting and worthwhile, too. For the best of Sangiovese, go for Isole e Olena, Querciabella, Monte Vertine and Frescobaldi. Little is made outside Italy, although the Californians show the most interest and produce one or two excellent examples, such as Seghesio's old-vine example, and straight varietal wines from Flora Springs and Il Podere dell' Olivos.

## TEMPRANILLO

Just as Sangiovese is the great grape of Italy's most famous red wine, so Tempranillo is the main variety behind Spain's most lauded wine, Rioja. The Rioja region in northwest Spain has been making distinctive, oak-aged reds for over a century. Don't make the common mistake of thinking that red Rioja is big, heavy and tannic. It is mellow, smooth, aged at the *bodega* (winery) in cask

and then bottled so that it's ready to drink on release. The typical flavours are cream and vanilla (from long ageing in American oak, which gives more of this character than French oak) and hints of aromatic, sweetly ripe strawberry fruit. Garnacha plays an important part in some blends, and smaller amounts of the Spanish grapes Graciano (which provides structure and tannin) and Mazuelo (aka Carignan, for colour and body) are often used as well. In a small number of blends, Cabernet Sauvignon has been successfully brought in, though these wines are officially just 'experiments'.

There are several categories of red Rioja, according to the length of oak-ageing. A few cheaper, less interesting wines will be young (*joven*), unoaked (*sin crianza*) or very lightly oaked (*semi-crianza*), but all serious, traditional Rioja will have seen the inside of an oak barrel for a significant period of time.

*Crianza* on a label indicates a year in oak, and further bottle-age before release; a *reserva* requires three years' ageing, at least one of which must be in cask and another in bottle; and *gran reserva* means five years' maturation, at least two in bottle and two in cask. Each of these last three groups is worthwhile. *Crianza* is the liveliest of the trio, with more sprightly fresh, red-berry fruit; *reserva* starts to show velvety smoothness and mellow flavours; and *gran reserva* should be a wine of great maturity, depth and roundness.

Variations on the theme include those Cabernet blends, wines with more rich, tannic characteristics, and wines that have been aged in French oak; but to many fans, red Rioja is all about soft, creamy oak and bags of strawberry aroma and flavour. That means American oak, long ageing and the Sangiovese grape. But to make sure you get a bottle you like, it pays to learn the house style of several different *bodegas*, and watch out for those categories of ageing described on the label. The best *bodegas* include El Coto, Marqués de Griñón, La Rioja Alta, López de Heredia, Martínez-Bujanda, Marqués de Riscal, Bodegas Roda, Palacio Marqués de Murrieta and Muga. Great recent vintages: 2001, 1999, 1996, 1995, 1994, and 1991.

## NERO D'AVOLA, PRIMITIVO, NEGROAMARO AND MONTEPULCIANO

Here are four more Italian grapes (this country is clearly a maestro when it comes to medium-bodied reds). The first three hail from much further south, where they are the local varieties that lie behind many of Italy's new-wave, inexpensive reds. Puglia is the most important region for decent wines made from the grape Negroamaro – expect soft, moreish, plummy reds, and plain chocolate hints – though you might try the appellation of Salice Salentino, too. Primitivo is thought to be the same grape as Zinfandel, which makes big, gutsy reds in California (see page 98). Montepulciano makes lots of fresh and easy-drinking red in central and southeast Italy. In short, many Italian reds are agreeably easy-going, medium-bodied and food-friendly. Few are truly light or heavily rich. Italian reds make a good choice for matching with food especially as many have a fresh, cherry-sour lift at the end of the flavour which seems to cut through fatty dishes well.

## PERIQUITA

Portugal is currently enjoying a new wave of popularity for its cheap, but pleasant reds from the central regions of the country. These are smooth and juicy with cherry, strawberry and red plum flavours although they need drinking up while they are still young. Periquita

is the variety behind many of these wines, which are a sensible, low-budget choice for pleasing a crowd at a party. Supermarkets usually stock fair Portuguese reds made from Periquita at low prices.

## CINSAULT

I can't pretend to be a big fan of Cinsault, which often makes uninspiring reds in southern France and rather rough ones in South Africa (where it is spelt Cinsaut). But it has its fans, particularly for the occasional new-wave wines that have been made from the grapes of low-yielding old vines.

## DOLCETTO AND BARBERA

These are two grapes grown in Piedmont, northern Italy, that live in the shadow of the more famous local grape Nebbiolo, and are not hugely well-known outside Italy. Well worth seeking out, both provide better-than-average, highly food-friendly wine and rarely disappoint. Dolcetto (the 'little sweet one') makes soft wines with a succulent, red-cherry flavour and plenty of acidity – even a slightly sour twist on the end. This helps the wine to cut through fatty food, and Dolcetto is a star turn with rich, meaty pasta sauces or cheesy pasta bakes. It has been described as the Gamay (Beaujolais grape) of northern Italy, although I tend to think it is better than that, and can make some excellent, intensely fruity wines, some of which descend into delicious chocolatey depths. Top labels are Domenico Clerico, Bruno Giacosa, Gaja, Mascarello and Voerzio.

There is less argument today about the sophistication of premium Barbera, plummy and fresh yet ripe and satisfying. Those who find Nebbiolo, the grape behind Barolo and Barbaresco (see page 96), too much like hard work, should go for Barbera. It used to be seen as the source of everyday, straightforward reds, but in the last fifteen years or so some producers (many the same as those named above for Nebbiolo) have taken it more seriously, planting it in better sites, cutting back on the fruit yields, using fine oak barrels to age it. Some of the resulting wines have shown Barbera make the leap to a first-rate red.

## MEDIUM MALBEC

Most Malbecs fall into the next category, so see page 96, 'Full-bodied Reds', for more detail here, but Argentina's key red grape does produce some easy-going, mellow, softer wines which are distinctly medium-bodied in style. These offer some lovely ripe cherry and plum flavours and slip down easily as decent party reds or as all-purpose dinner wines that go well with pasta in meat sauces, red meat or vegetarian bakes. Loosely speaking, the cheaper Malbecs tend to be the slightly lighter wines.

# MAKING THE DIFFERENCE

ONE FACTOR THAT INFLUENCES THE CHARACTER OF MEDIUM-BODIED REDS IS THE SORT OF OAK-AGEING THEY RECEIVE. Some of the wines described in this chapter are not aged in oak at all, and have a more immediate, simple, fresh-fruit flavour. This may be true of the southern Italian reds, Portuguese Periquita, some lighter Merlots, and Rioja *sin crianza* ('without oak'), for example. Other wines spend time in barrel, picking up nuances of vanilla, cream and hints of spice and cedar along the way. The majority of Bordeaux reds, California Merlots, and Chianti Classicos are barrel-aged. Top Pomerols in particular should have a fine, well-balanced oaky layer of complexity. Rioja is matured for years and it is traditionally kept in vanilla-rich, American-oak casks to pick up its characteristic mellow, creamy flavour and softness.

# MATCHING MEDIUM-BODIED SOFT REDS WITH FOOD

EASY! THE MEDIUM-BODIED REDS GO WITH A WIDE RANGE OF SAVOURY DISHES. They don't have heavy tannins, sharp acidity or excess sugar (or they shouldn't have), which means there is little to clash with the food. Just avoid striking the wrong balance. Don't match medium-bodied reds with very light dishes – leafy salads and grilled white fish are out – as they will overpower the food, and don't crack open a bottle to go with a very hearty stew or heavily spiced meat dish, as the wine won't stand up to it. Otherwise, the choice is yours. Game birds, roast poultry, pork and ham, pasta in meaty sauces, roast vegetables, medium hard cheeses, grilled steaks, hamburgers, pizzas, sausages, shepherd's pie are all good bets. Oh, and Rioja is brilliant with grilled lamb chops and garlic!

# STORING AND SERVING

THE MEDIUM REDS SHOULD NOT BE KEPT FOR MANY YEARS UNLESS THEY ARE THE STRIKING, CONCENTRATED, EXPENSIVE TOP WINES OF BORDEAUX, CALIFORNIA AND ITALY. These majestic bottles can be cellared for many years and they become more drinkable, softer and more mellow with time. But no-nonsense, everyday softies should be enjoyed within one year of purchase or they will start to lose their vibrant berry fruit flavour. Red Rioja is aged in barrel, then in the bottle at the bodega (winery), and is released ready to drink. Do not age it for years or it might start to taste tired. Serve all the wines described in this chapter at room temperature, in big wine glasses so you can swirl the liquid around and release those lovely fruity aromas.

# FIRST TASTE

■ RED FRUITS RULE HERE! Expect masses of strawberry, cherry and red plums. If your medium red lacks fruity character, there's something wrong with it.

■ The body and structure should be well-balanced – neither too light and jammy, nor too heavy and tannic. THESE REDS ARE MEANT TO BE ROUNDED, SILKY AND RELATIVELY EASY TO DRINK when young.

■ Beware the green, stalky medium red. This means the grapes were not ready when they were picked. SMOOTH, JUICY REDS CANNOT BE MADE FROM UNDERRIPE GRAPES. Avoid that label in the future.

■ LOOK OUT FOR CHOCOLATEY NOTES IN MANY OF THESE WINES. They are not just about red fruit, but often about a choccy, creamy, vanilla roundness, too.

■ And MANY HAVE A TANGY FINISH, ENDING ON A MOUTH-WATERING NOTE, or even a slightly tart note. This is especially true of the medium-bodied Italian reds, and, if the tartness is not over-done, it means the wines cut through rich food well.

# BUYER'S GUIDE

■ The top Merlot-rich wines from Bordeaux (St-Emilion, Pomerol) and the finest California Merlots and Merlot/ Cabernets are extremely expensive. SOME OF THEM ARE MAGNIFICENT, THE APOGEE OF THIS STYLE, but you will rarely find a bargain. These are cult wines.

■ But don't go to the other extreme and buy the very cheapest claret (red Bordeaux). This is often Merlot at its most mundane. SPEND A LITTLE MORE TO SAMPLE DECENT BORDEAUX. Or go for Vin de Pays d'Oc Merlot for a reliable cheapie. Likewise, avoid basic California Merlot, which can be sweetish, over-oaky and unsubtle.

■ CHILEAN MERLOT IS GREAT VALUE FOR MONEY: fruity, easy-drinking, soft and friendly. It's consistent, too, with bags of plummy flavour and chocolate. Don't miss it.

■ South Africa is making some of the most impressive Merlot and Merlot blends for a fair price. SNAP UP SOUTH AFRICAN MERLOT before the Cape starts to charge more for such good wine.

■ GREAT, EVERYDAY, MEDIUM-BODIED GLUGGERS INCLUDE WINES FROM PUGLIA in southern Italy and Periquita in Portugal, with red berries and soft texture.

# MOVING ON

■ TRY MERLOT FROM UNUSUAL SOURCES – Sicily, Austria or New Zealand, for example – to see how its place of origin shapes its character. This is a well-travelled grape that is made all over the winemaking world.

■ SAMPLE THE RANGE OF STYLES THIS GRAPE MAKES, from light, refreshing northern Italian Merlots, to fruit-driven, warm-climate bottles, to the chunkier, more serious Bordeaux wines.

■ DOLCETTO AND BARBERA ARE MUST-HAVES FROM ITALY: two grape varieties from Piedmont with wonderful cherry and plum flavours. If you like better-known Chianti, then give these wines a go.

■ Chianti Classico and Rioja reserva are extremely food-friendly (the first from Tuscany, the second from northern Spain). CHIANTI AND RIOJA ARE BOTH GREAT CHOICES WHEN DINING, and often reasonably priced.

■ Rioja fans, BE AWARE THAT THERE ARE DIFFERENT TYPES OF RED RIOJA ACCORDING TO THE AMOUNT OF TIME MATURED IN OAK; also some wines are aged in French oak, not traditional American casks, and some are made with the addition of Cabernet. NOT ALL RIOJA TASTES THE SAME!

THE FULL-BODIED REDS ARE NOT FOR THE FAINT-HEARTED. They fill your mouth with rich fruit and tannin, spice and oak, and the flavours and textures seem to linger long after they have been swallowed. Younger wines tend to be chewier and firmer; older ones are gentler and more mellow while retaining concentrated fruit and intensity. Poor ones are either too dilute and jammy or they are unbalanced – too much oak, too much tannin, too much sweetly ripe, 'in-yer-face' cassis flavour. Watch out for wines that impress on first taste, but which you wouldn't drink in any quantity. These are often referred to as 'show wines'; they win awards for their extra clout, but don't always make enjoyable drinking.

That said, if you generally prefer lighter reds, think twice before writing off richer, more full-bodied wines. Like so many styles, but perhaps even more so here, they should be cracked open at exactly the right moment to be appreciated fully, not brought out on every occasion. For example, blockbuster reds do not make great party wines. They are neither soft nor mellow enough to slip down without food; that big-framed tannic structure may only make sense with a forkful of a rare steak. Similarly, they do not suit hot weather, or outdoor wining and dining. Although they might match a barbecued meat fest, their high alcohol and richness can be a quick route to a headache. Stick to medium or light styles of red on a picnic or at a party.

So, bring out the heavyweights to partner robust winter dishes: peppery stews, roast red meats, cheeseboards and rich vegetarian bakes. Used carefully, these make the ultimate comfort wines: soothing and contentment-enducing. Some age well, too, so cellar-owners should take note of what follows. The big reds are like all hefty and daunting things in life: potentially overwhelming but wonderful when handled correctly.

## TEXTURE

Tannin – the substance that gives wine a lot of rich body and structure, and an almost 'chewy' mouth feel, like sucking on a wooden pencil – can feature heavily here, especially in younger bottles. Other wines have a more rounded quality, but retain that rich weightiness in the mouth.

## APPEARANCE

Dark red, ranging from a port-like, concentrated garnet to brighter, richly purple and even damson-black. Most look intense, dense in colour if you hold a glassful up to the light. Younger wines tend to be a more bluey-purple; older ones are brick-brown.

## AROMA

The fruit aromas tend to be blackcurrant and blackberry, sometimes very pungent, like a whiff of crème de cassis. Hints of toffee, spice, black pepper, eucalyptus, tar, treacle, liquorice and mint sometimes feature. Very oaky wines have a strong vanilla character, even sawdust-like on the nose.

## FLAVOUR

Fruit flavours include an intense blackcurrant akin to black fruit gums – also briar fruits, brambles, and raspberries in certain wines. Look out, too, for a twist of spice (cloves, cinnamon) and especially black pepper on the finish; chocolate, spicy vanillins and chewy tannins, too. Older wines have a leather or suede character.

# CABERNET SAUVIGNON

## THE 'KING' OF RED GRAPES

Cabernet is often referred to as the 'king' of red grapes. Why? It's astonishingly popular among consumers and winemakers, it is grown all over the world and, in most places, it makes at least good, and often great, wine. In terms of reliability it reigns supreme – most Cabernet is palatable, and complete duds are relatively rare. It often makes firm and full-bodied reds capable of long ageing, it takes well to maturation in French-oak barrels, picking up aromatic hints of cedar and vanilla, and it blends well with other varieties, particularly Merlot and Shiraz. This is one red grape with which winemakers aspire to make their greatest wines.

The main attributes of top Cabernet are its wonderfully concentrated cassis character, its firm structure and effortless ageing ability. Look out for the former when you sip this wine. A good example will not only ooze blackcurrant but may well have complex undertones of mint, plain chocolate, lead pencil, cedar and fresh cigars. That may sound a bit fanciful, but this is one deep and meaningful grape, and tasters find all sorts of nuances in there. With age (in the wine, not the taster!), they spot leather, game, marmite, earth... Let your inner poet go wild when you describe Cabernet to yourself.

That rich, often tannic structure is derived from the fact that the Cabernet vine forms thick-skinned, small-berried grapes with a high proportion of skin and pips compared to the amount of juice they contain. This produces wine with plenty of rich, purple colour and high levels of tannin. It also explains the reason why certain wines age well, their tannins softening over time. Blending Cabernet with some other fleshier grapes – Merlot, for example – fills out this somewhat tough flavour with more approachable fruitiness.

# FRANCE

Red Bordeaux, or claret, may be disappointing at the cheaper end of the market, but few would dispute that top examples remain some of the most serious and exciting red wines in the world. Although Merlot plantings exceed Cabernet in Bordeaux, it can be argued that the latter rules in the region. Red Bordeaux still spells Cabernet for most drinkers – Cabernet filled out by Merlot and Cabernet Franc in the blend, but essentially Cabernet in all its venerable, aromatic, cassis-drenched glory, almost sweetly ripe, dry on the finish, the ripe fruit held up by a firm structure of tannins.

But the world of wine is never straightforward. In truth, a lot of inexpensive clarets rely on Merlot more heavily; the worst tend towards jammy, dilute dross, while in the great Merlot estates of St-Emilion and Pomerol (see pages 46–49), Cabernet plays a very minor role in the blend. But in the Médoc, on the left bank of the Gironde, close to the Atlantic and protected by the forests of Les Landes, Cabernet is the main player in some of the most sought-after and well-loved wines of all – those from the villages of the Haut-Médoc: Margaux, St-Julien, Pauillac and St-Estèphe. Here the vines grow in well-drained, gravel soils near to the Gironde estuary. Some of the glitteringly famous chateaux of Haut-Médoc are Château Margaux (Margaux); Léoville-Barton, Gruaud-Larose (St-Julien), Latour, Lafite, Mouton-Rothschild (Pauillac) and Cos d'Estournel (St-Estèphe). Expect very high prices indeed for these much sought-after wines.

Another part of the region where Cabernet is dominant is the Graves, closer to the city of Bordeaux. The best wines come from the Pessac-Léognan area of Graves, and include the first-growth Haut-Brion. First growth? The Bordeaux classification system is something that all traditional wine buffs make an effort to master, even though it sometimes seems ludicrously old-fashioned and out of touch. It works on a pyramid structure with five tiers of *crus classés* (classed growths). The most important summary of rankings was made in 1855. (See what I mean about outmoded?) Today there is much controversy over which *châteaux* deserve demotion and promotion. For example, some fifth-growth *châteaux*, such as Lynch-Bages and Grand-Puy-Lacoste, make superb wines that belie their relatively low ranking. Make your own mind up by trying as many as possible (though let's hope you are being treated, as prices for top clarets are, of course, sky-high). Those who are impressed by famous classed-growth labels should note that ninety per cent of wine made in the commune of Pauillac is classed growth, and its *châteaux* Latour, Lafite and Mouton-Rothschild are all first growths. It should be said that some of these wines are truly remarkable in terms of complexity, depth of flavour, fine balance and longevity. Then again, some wonder what all the fuss is about. The only answer is to try out fine claret and see what you think.

For those of us who haven't won the lottery, the Médoc region of Bordeaux also produces plenty of generic red wine for a much lower outlay. Here's a useful hint: try wines labelled 'Cru Bourgeois', the category just below classed growth. Within this group, the many *châteaux* are well worth a whirl and often offer some fine drinking at a reasonable price. Or try the 'second wines' of the great *châteaux*, made either from rejected blends of the top houses or from the fruit of young, up-and-coming vines. Taste Les Forts de Latour or Pavillon Rouge from Château Margaux, among others – not exactly cheap, but cheaper.

When buying both these good-value wines and the classed growths, it's important to choose a decent vintage: these not only taste better when young, they age better, too. Recent fine vintages include 2000, 1997 (for earlier drinking), 1995, 1990, 1989 and 1988. For more on the slightly lighter generic clarets and Merlot-heavy blends from the region, see the section on 'Medium-bodied, Soft Reds' (pages 38–69).

Bergerac makes a few wines from the Cabernet grape that are relatively full-bodied, but in general they are softer than in Bordeaux's most famous areas. Some rich Cabernets and Cabernet blends can be found more widely in southwest France, including thick, ripe modern wines from the Languedoc. Generally, these tend to lack the subtlety and ageing potential of the top clarets, with a 'New World' sunny, blackcurrant flavour, but can be good value if you want a modern, fruit-driven wine.

# REST OF EUROPE

Spain has proved it can make some impressive Cabernet, mainly in Penedès (thank you, Miguel Torres and Jean León, who pioneered international grapes here), although plenty of other regions are now throwing Cabernet into the blend. In Rioja and Ribera del Duero, progressive winemakers blend it with the main variety Tempranillo for some successful, ripe reds, while Navarra makes some fruity, straightforward, single-varietal Cabs. Ribera's Vega Sicilia makes one of the most famous Spanish reds of all: a long-lived blend of Tempranillo, Cabernet, Merlot and Malbec.

It's a similar story in Italy, where winemakers tend to use Cabernet to make interesting, premium blends with Merlot or the Tuscan grape, Sangiovese. The variety is becoming increasingly important in central Italy, where many serious, concentrated reds are based on Cabernet. This means that the wines fall foul of the local regulations (Cabernet isn't allowed) and therefore can't attain normal DOCG status. These wild-card wines, known as 'Super-Tuscans', are much admired by collectors of fine Italian reds. The most famous are made by the Antinori winery.

Eastern Europe, and particularly Bulgaria, is known for cheap-and-cheerful Cabernet. No longer as popular an everyday glugger as it once was, Bulgarian Cabernet can still be pleasant, with clean cassis fruit, a rounded texture and some creamy oak in most examples. These wines are a bit 'mass-market', however, fairly boring, and not quite as rich as one might hope for. Still, they are doggedly cheap. Domaine Boyar is the name to go for if you want to try a Bulgarian Cabernet.

Finally, perhaps surprisingly, Austria is source of decent Cabernet, usually in the form of blends with Merlot and sometimes local Austrian grapes. The Burgenland region makes the majority of worthwhile examples.

## REST OF THE WORLD

In newer wine-producing regions, more premium wines are made from Cabernet than from any other grape. Many winemakers here aspire to a 'flagship' wine that is produced from pure Cabernet or, more usually, a classic Bordeaux blend. This variety travels well, producing fine wine in many sites, as long as there is enough heat for it to ripen sufficiently, as this is a slow developer, and also providing soils don't get too wet. It generally obliges, coming up with that signature cassis in warm southern hemisphere countries, usually a particularly ripe and juicy note, and plenty of colour and body.

Of course, there are exceptions, and those pursuing warm-climate Cabernet should be aware that

blandness can be a problem. Simple, fruity, one-dimensional wines are all very well – if you don't give a hoot for the fact that this grape is capable of so much more. Cabernet is now so overwhelmingly popular that some wineries churn it out as a cheap, commercial wine because putting this grape on a label means it will sell. It's easy to get bored with these wines, and inevitably some wise drinkers will switch to more exciting, if lesser-known, varieties. So watch out – reasonably palatable just isn't good enough from this great grape!

Argentina has been guilty of making Cabernets like this for the past few years and although a few decent examples are made here, there are more exciting Argentinian reds to be had from the Malbec and Syrah grapes (for the latter, see pages 88–93). Neighbouring Chile is much more exciting when it comes to Cabernet. A fine, classic example of Chilean Cabernet strikes a memorably pure, clear, bright blackcurrant note – like eating a big spoonful of shiny fruit from a baked currant pie. Take into account the low prices of many bottles, and it's easy to see why the Chilean style is immensely popular. Rapel is one region to look out for, and some of the top labels from Chile are made by Errázuriz, Santa Rita and Santa Carolina. It is in the mid-price bracket where this style truly excels; cheapies can sometimes be a bit mundane, and Chile has yet to prove it can make truly great, top-rank Cabernet and Cabernet blends in significant numbers.

Further north, California is the source of some monster Cabernets – monster in the sense of big, brooding, ultra-concentrated wines with loads of extract and decades of life ahead of them. These are wines to take seriously; the top ones can rival Bordeaux in terms of complexity and longevity, although it can be argued that they are a little less subtle, and major in thick, rich fruit and vanilla rather than anything else. Unsurprisingly, they are very expensive and are often snapped up by rich American collectors, who squirrel them away in cellars for years. The best come from the Napa Valley, Sonoma and some sites south of San Francisco Bay; coolish hillside sites producing the most interesting wines. Watch out for some heavily alcoholic and unbalanced numbers, although thankfully these have diminished in recent years and it seems that quality is on the up. Producers to go for include Beringer, Caymus, Hess Collection, Mondavi, Opus One, Joseph Phelps and Screaming Eagle (though strictly for millionnaires). Try Washington State's Cabernet, too – it's beginning to show great promise, with wines tasting intensely fruity.

Australia's best reds are made from Shiraz – a personal view, but there you go. Still, its Cabernet comes a close second. Basic cheap blends of Cabernet and Shiraz can be a bit boring and bland, but more serious examples – you have to spend more – tend to be flavour-packed and chunky. Cabernet on its own varies in character from region to region, which will surprise those who think all Aussie wine tastes the same!

So, Coonawarra is an area well worth exploring, its famous 'terra rossa' iron-rich soils providing exciting, elegant wines which are nonetheless packed with fruit and firm structure. Padthaway, Clare Valley and McLaren Vale give different interpretations; look out for notes of chocolate, eucalyptus, blackberry and wine gums, and make up your own mind about which regional style you prefer. Margaret River, south of Perth in the west, makes particularly compelling, subtle-yet-powerful Cabernet and Cabernet blends. Top producers from across the country include Penfolds, Cullen, Leeuwin

Estate, Chapel Hill and Yalumba. Look out, too, for some excellent, gutsy wines from South Africa. A few years ago, Cape Cabernet and Cabernet blends looked much less promising as many vineyards were diseased. Dull, fruitless, tired wines were all too often the experience. Now, virus-free clones have matured and, in general, South African winemaking has wised up to overseas competition and started to compete more cleverly. The future is looking bright. The warmer Stellenbosch region is clearly the best for Cabernet, with Paarl vineyards a close second. Top labels to try out include Clos Malverne, Vergelegen, De Toren, De Trafford, Grangehurst, Plaisir de Merle and Rustenberg.

That covers the major Cabernet-producing countries, but Cabernet hunters should look out for the occasional gem from New Zealand – with Bordeaux-style blends of Cabernet and Merlot, sometimes with Cabernet Franc and Malbec, from the Hawke's Bay region of the North Island currently the most successful formula. And then there's the Lebanon, where one winery, Château Musar, puts out a blend of Cabernet with the lesser-known Cinsault grape which has become a rich, leathery, spicy cult red. A must if you are exploring this variety – although not to everyone's taste.

# SYRAH/SHIRAZ

A WALK ON THE WILD SIDE

Syrah and Shiraz are one and the same grape variety – Syrah is the French name, and Shiraz is the name given to it in Australia, South Africa and other parts of the world. This grape variety is a must if you want to experience the richer, darker side of red wine. Not all Syrahs/Shirazes (or blends that incorporate it) will be satisfyingly full-on, so watch out for some of the weedy, jammy cheapies, but in the main, this is one of the grapes to go for if you want a heavyweight. It doesn't often deliver fresh, fruity flavours, however.

Syrah/Shiraz can be lots of things, but it isn't in the 'fruit salad' school of wine. It's hard to swirl a glass of the stuff and find raspberries, strawberries, plums and cassis, as you will with many red grapes. Instead, potent, wilder aromas assail the nostrils – of spice, black pepper, toffee, cream, herbs, smoke, leather, citrus peel – and the taste is similar. Sure, there is a rich blackberry/

blackcurrant element in certain, especially non-European, Shirazes, but those unusual characteristics still stand out, and are what make this grape so misunderstood and often underrated. It was often used as a 'workhorse', churning out cheap and rough reds, especially in Australia, until the modern era kicked in and winemakers started making first-rate, premium reds from it. Those who liked powerful, robust wines loved Shiraz; a modern classic was born.

Of course, as Syrah, this grape was always much appreciated. The Rhône Valley is renowned for its gutsy, concentrated, sun-baked reds, and Syrah has always played a major part in these. This variety's popularity is set to grow as more winemakers around the world take it on and come up with startlingly good results. Still, for now it remains less well-known than Cabernet, Merlot and Pinot Noir. So, if you haven't discovered Syrah/Shiraz yet, make a point of doing so now. Note it is made in the warmer parts of the winemaking globe, where the hot sun coaxes the grapes into ripeness.

## FRANCE

The huge, smouldering reds of the northern Rhône Valley are made almost entirely from Syrah. This is a sunny area that starts at Vienne, with the appellation of Côte-Rôtie ('roasted slope'), and runs southwards to St-Péray, near the town of Valence. The wines are dense, intense, super-concentrated with a twist of black pepper and a rich, rounded texture. Some have a sprinkling of white Viognier grapes in the blend, which gives the liquid a fragant lift. The winemakers of Côte-Rôtie are arguably the greatest in the south, making brooding monsters packed with black fruit and spice, but don't pass up the chance for a decent bottle from the appellations of Crozes-Hermitage, Hermitage, St-Joseph and Cornas,

either. Names such as Chapoutier, Chave, Graillot, Delas, Guigal and Paul Jaboulet are all well worth exploring. The best wines are thoroughly age worthy, their heavy structure softening and loosening up over time.

The southern section of the Rhône begins below Montélimar and is a hot, arid place where rich, headily alcoholic reds are the norm. The most famous wine of the region is the purple-hued, heavyweight Châteauneuf-du-Pape, which is made from a heady mix of up to thirteen different grape varieties, mainly Grenache (see page 94) but also Syrah and Mourvèdre. Vineyards contain big flat stones which retain the heat of the sun well into the evening. Other southern Rhône reds produced from a similar blend include Gigondas, Vacqueyras and Lirac. Again, the top wines should mature well for years. Further down the prestige ladder come sixteen named Côtes du Rhône-Villages (including Cairanne, Rasteau and Beaumes-de-Venise), then generic Côtes du Rhône-Villages, which are often good value for money, and below that the cheapish Côtes du Rhône reds, which can occasionally please but are often basic and a bit dilute. Château de Beaucastel, Château Rayas and Vieux Télégraphe are all top labels. In the south of France, Syrah is often used in blends or on its own to make modern, flavoursome reds with a black-wine-gum flavour – these will appeal to lovers of non-European Shiraz and Cabernet.

## AUSTRALIA

This is the country that relied on Shiraz (as they call it) as a trusty servant for over a century, turning out fortified wine and basic 'dry reds' from it until finally realising it could (and should) be taken far more seriously. Now it is one of Australia's trump cards, producing some of its most awesome wines, much from ancient vines which yield small harvests of wonderfully concentrated grapes. The result is big, powerful, mouth-filling red wine, heavy on the black-fruit pastilles, chewy and lingering, smooth and often velvety in its flavour – the gentle giants of the red-wine world. Australian Shiraz is reliable, too – you will rarely encounter a complete horror, so if you like this style of wine, you are on to a good thing. Blends of Shiraz with Cabernet produce some rather mundane, soft reds, but other compellingly rich bins.

The most famous Aussie Shiraz is Penfolds' Grange. It's an amazingly long-lived, intense red made mainly from fruit grown in the hot Barossa Valley, South Australia, one of the best sources of Shiraz in the country. Grange is not cheap, to put it mildly. In the Hunter Valley, New South Wales, Shiraz has a reputation for being leathery and with an aroma

of 'sweaty saddles', but the vaguely grubby styles of the past have made way for cleaner, fruitier wines. McLaren Vale Shiraz can be honest, big, chocolatey stuff, Victoria makes peppery, perfumed variants, and Western Australia makes cassis-laden wines with subtle nuances of eucalyptus and mint. Look out for these and other regional characteristics. Which names should you watch for? Top labels include Penfolds, Hardy's top wines, Peter Lehmann, Henschke, Jasper Hill, Charles Melton, Mount Langi Ghiran, Tatachilla, Yalumba and Jim Barry, but cheaper own-label brands can be tasty, too.

## REST OF THE WORLD

This is currently a fashionable variety, and winemakers are embracing it in many countries, so watch this space as more fine examples appear on the shelves. In California, producers who love Rhône varieties have been dubbed the 'Rhône Rangers' – sample the efforts of Bonny Doon, or Cline Cellars to judge how well they are doing. South Africa is one to watch; some of the Syrah/Shiraz coming out of the Cape at the moment is marvellously concentrated and Rhône-like, with a strong, oaky structure. Try wines from the Groot Constantia and Boekenhoutskloof wineries if you get the chance. New Zealand is a surprising source of fine Syrah – surprising because this grape needs lots of warmth and it doesn't get too hot there. But the sunny Hawke's Bay region is proving it can be successful with this variety. More plantings are set to come on stream in the next few years, so look out for Kiwi Syrah. Another tip is Argentina where wines from the Mendoza region, close to the Andes, are causing a stir for their ripe, smooth character.

# OTHER FULL-BODIED REDS

## PLENTY MORE TO PICK FROM

### GRENACHE

The Grenache grape doesn't excel at making subtle, complex, elegant reds: oh, no. This variety makes big, boisterous, joyful wines with high alcohol levels, although relatively low tannins. It tastes of sweet, plummy fruit, sometimes with a hint of chocolate and it has a dry but succulent finish. It has been used and abused in the past to make cheap-and-cheerless, disappointingly dilute wine from irrigated, high-yielding vines, but in recent years there's been a movement towards premium Grenache with loads more flavour, body and guts.

Find it in the south of France, in the Languedoc, in the southern Rhône (as a major component of Châteauneuf-du-Pape, see page 90) and all along the French coast of the Med. It is often blended with Syrah and Mourvèdre. Some Australians take it seriously, particularly Charles Melton in the Barossa Valley, and the Californians are starting to show interest. But the most important country after France for this grape is Spain, where, as Garnacha, it is making increasingly serious and concentrated, powerful reds, usually from old vines. The scenic mountain region of Priorato is the place to go for the serious

monsters, although Tarragona comes a close second. Expect massive wines which may need years to open up. Alvaro Palacios, Clos Erasmus and Clos Mogador are some of the wineries you should look out for.

## NEBBIOLO

Nebbiolo is the grape behind Italy's huge Piedmont reds, Barolo and Barbaresco. It ripens late in the autumn, in the mist-covered hills of the region (hence the name Nebbiolo, which means 'foggy'), and it makes a dense wine with high levels of acid and tannin. There's nothing else quite like Nebbiolo, which has a savoury yet floral perfume (some spot roses) and hints of truffles, blackberry and liquorice. Many consider it to be a truly great variety. Certainly, top examples are impressive, refreshingly different and they also age brilliantly. Nebbiolo is hardly ever made elsewhere, partly because mastering

its high acidity and thick tannin, while prising some fruity character out, is so difficult. Aldo Conterno, Gaja, Roberto Voerzio and Giacosa are all Italian masters. Prices for the well-known producers are high and you need to beware any really poor vintages. Another hefty Italian that is worth a try is Amarone from Valpolicella, made from the juice of dried grapes (mostly Corvina). It is gloriously thick, ripe and alcoholic and makes a great accompaniment to cheese.

## MALBEC

Argentina's greatest success to date has been with the Malbec grape, which originally comes from Cahors but has become a minor vine in France. Immigrants planted it long ago in the Mendoza region and today it produces beautifully rich but rounded, smooth reds packed with black-cherry fruit. It goes brilliantly with steak, and quality is high from many producers.

## TANNAT

Uruguay's ace card, according to its fans. Tannat is a thick-skinned, sturdy grape, which produces leathery, highly tannic wines with mulberry fruit and toffee-rich depths. Uruguay is still fairly unknown to most wine-drinkers, but as more of its producers start to export, look out for Tannat, which does well in the damp maritime climate of this South American country. Not all bottles will please – there are too many over-chewy, tannic, thick-set examples – but it can be deliciously different. Tannat's original home is Madiran in southern France, where it again makes very tannic, almost black wine which will appeal to lovers of rich reds, but which need at least a decade in bottle before they start to open up.

## BAGA AND TOURIGA NACIONAL

Two Portuguese varieties which are capable of making the most interesting and complex reds in the country. Baga is found mainly in Bairrada in northern Portugal, and is a tough grape with a thick skin which produces (you guessed it) tannic, powerful wines. In the past, many of these proved too hard and heavy-going, but modern vinification methods are turning up a new generation of Bairrada reds with softer blackberry and liquorice flavours. Try Luis Pato's wines.

Touriga Nacional is found in port country, and is perhaps the most hallowed of all the port grapes. Today it is the mainstay of the Dão region and the new, often brilliant, unfortified red wines coming out of the Douro Valley, the best of which are bursting with intense flavours of red fruit and blackcurrant, and have plenty of rounded but firm structure. These wines age well. Good examples to try are Quinta de la Rosa and Quinta do Crasto, among others.

## PINOTAGE

A South African grape developed by crossing Pinot Noir and Cinsault. There used to be a spooky amount of rough, sour, tomatoey Pinotage knocking around, but quality has improved dramatically as Cape winemakers get on top of modern methods, and many more ripe, plummy, carefully oaked wines are now appearing. Cheap Pinotage can be simple stuff, fruity and medium-bodied, but top examples are concentrated, creamily rich and very satisfying. Kanonkop is the most famous producer, but try Longridge, Beyerskloof, Simonsig and Warwick Estate, too. Great with barbecued red meats – so light the braii!

## ZINFANDEL

Californian wine can get rather boring with its flood of predictably oaky, rich Chardonnays and Cabernets, so here's a welcome and refreshing change. Zinfandel ('Zin') is a West Coast speciality capable of making generously fruity, full-bodied, often highly alcoholic, reds with a thick, sweetly ripe, raspberry flavour and a twist of black pepper. Most believe that it is the same grape as Italy's Primitivo and was brought over by Italian immigrants. Watch out for a few overblown, over-oaky monsters, but always avoid bland pink and off-white Zin in favour of red. Best producers: Ridge, Seghesio, Frog's Leap and Fetzer Bonterra.

# MAKING THE DIFFERENCE

THE FULL-BODIED, ALMOST MOUTH-COATING TEXTURE OF THE WORLD'S BIGGEST REDS COMES FROM TANNIN, WHICH IS A SUBSTANCE FOUND IN THE SKINS, PIPS AND STALKS OF GRAPES. Tannins are a group of complex organic substances also found in bark and other fruits. Tannin from pips is bitter, so canny winemakers take care to avoid crushing the seeds. Some avoid using stems in the mix as well, although others think they benefit the finished wine. The skins provide more benevolent tannins and plenty of colour, too. Powerful reds are made from small berries with thick skins so their concentration of tannin and colour is higher than average. The grapes must be ripe, or a nasty, furry, green tannic character is the result. Extra tannin is added when a wine is aged in new-oak barrels, which leach some of their wood character into the wine.

# MATCHING FULL-BODIED REDS WITH FOOD

DON'T SERVE THESE WINES ON THEIR OWN AS THEY ARE TOO HEAVY, and don't even think about matching them with light salads, fish or seafood (salted cod is the only exception), cold chicken, mild cheeses… the wines will walk all over the food and you will hardly taste your dinner. Instead, find a dish that is hearty enough to match your blockbuster wine. Roast red meats, rich stews, peppery steaks, full-flavoured cheeses and hot cheesy bakes are all good candidates. More specifically, match decent Médoc with roast lamb (the mint and blackcurrant of Cabernet complement lamb perfectly), Argentinian Malbec with steak (a modern classic in Buenos Aires), Syrah/Shiraz with game birds or beef casseroles, Barolo and Amarone with fine hard cheeses, Zinfandel with classic Christmas turkey and trimmings, and Pinotage with char-grilled barbecued meats.

# STORING AND SERVING

AVOID COMMITTING INFANTICIDE! TOO MANY DRINKERS BUY A FULL-BODIED RED AND CRACK IT OPEN WHEN IT IS FAR TOO YOUNG, ENDING UP WITH A TOUGH, CHEWY WINE IN THEIR GLASS INSTEAD OF A MATURE, MELLOW MOUTHFUL. Beware youthful claret, Barolo and Barbaresco, top Rhône reds and the most serious Australian reds in particular. They will age well for years, if not decades. Store them on their sides in a cool, dark place and leave them well alone. Cheaper wines tend to be made for earlier drinking: within a year or two of purchase. Serve them at room temperature and decant any very heavy reds, just like port, to open up their aroma, soften their texture and possibly remove any solid dregs that lurk at the bottom of the bottle.

# FIRST TASTE

■ Many of these wines can be described as fruity, but this certainly doesn't spell out the whole picture. MANY FULL-BODIED REDS ARE SPICY — BLACK PEPPER, CLOVES, CINNAMON AND NUTMEG — with whiffs of chocolate, cream and toffee, even liquorice and tar, savoury notes and herbs. Cabernet can be minty!

■ TANNIC REDS NEED FOOD — on their own the structure may seem a little too firm and chewy. The same wine with a steak may seem more balanced as it will work well with the rich protein in the food.

■ That said, SOME RICH REDS ARE OUT OF BALANCE, steak or no steak. Beware over-tannic reds smelling of freshly planed wood and tasting like chewing on tea bags. Ditch them for subtler wines with more poise.

■ TASTE THESE WINES AT ROOM TEMPERATURE, not cellar-cold and never fireside-warm.

■ Open them up way before tasting to let the wine breathe — however, THE MORE EFFECTIVE WAY TO GET A TOUGH RED TO SOFTEN AND MELLOW IS TO DECANT IT before drinking. And swirl it around in big glasses to release its aroma.

# BUYER'S GUIDE

■ Good news! THERE ARE PLENTY OF RELIABLE, WELL-PRICED FULL-BODIED REDS out there, including Chilean Cabernet, Australian Cabernet and Cabernet-Shiraz blends. Not dirt-cheap, perhaps, but with loads of food-friendly flavour and concentration for relatively little outlay.

■ VERY CHEAP HEFTY REDS ARE WORTH AVOIDING. Bargain reds, even those made from Shiraz and Cabernet, almost certainly won't deliver a big personality, and may be dilute, bland or jammy.

■ And TREAD MORE CAREFULLY WITH CLARET (RED BORDEAUX) AT LOWER PRICES. It only starts to get reliable in the mid-price range and over, and you still need to be sure to pick a good year, a reputable producer, a fine wine merchant…

■ The top clarets, finest Aussie Shirazes and Italian Barolos all need time, so stash them away for several years or they are a waste of money. DON'T CRACK OPEN EXPENSIVE, RICH REDS UNLESS YOU KNOW THEY WILL BE READY TO DRINK. Use a specialist wine merchant and take advice on individual fine wine purchases.

# MOVING ON

■ Once you've sampled one hundred per cent Cabernet and Shiraz, TRY THE BLENDS – most red Bordeaux, Australian Cab-Shiraz, Cabernet-Merlot from around the world – for different flavours, aromas and textures.

■ TRY WINES FROM AS MANY DIFFERENT PARTS OF THE RHÔNE VALLEY AS YOU CAN FIND – this is a fascinating, multi-faceted region with a wide variety of Syrah- and Grenache-based wines. Then head down to the south of France for some more big reds.

■ SET UP A COMPARATIVE TASTING OF OTHER GUTSY REDS – Zinfandel from California, Pinotage from South Africa, Malbec and Tannat from South America.

■ See how full-bodied reds start to lose their tannic grip and soften with age. Some wines, like Barolo or fine claret, are fascinating to watch in development. BUY A FEW BOTTLES OF THE SAME WINE AND OPEN ONE EVERY SIX MONTHS OR SO to track its evolution.

■ EXPERIMENT WITH MATCHING DISHES TO BIG REDS, as these are very food-friendly wines. Try red meat with young claret and game with older versions. Match peppery Syrah with slightly spicy dishes, and decide which is best with mature cheese or roast lamb.

ROSÉS **108**
137

THINK PINK. ROSE IS BACK IN VOGUE, AFTER A PERIOD OF BEING SEVERELY UNDERRATED. Nothing compares to a frosty-cold glass of fresh, cerise-coloured wine on a summer's day. Now more and more people are turned on to its charms – men as well as girls! Nonetheless, there are still a few sugary, bland, old-fashioned rosés out there, so it pays to know which ones to select.

Rosé can be made in three ways: red grapes are crushed and the skins left in with the juice for several hours until the colour and flavours have leached into the liquid, which is then fermented; or, for a lighter style, the juice is run off the skins straightaway and fermented; or, occasionally, red wine is blended with white. Because rosé is a fragile wine not built with the structure to last well, you may come across a lot of pink that is past its best and tastes dull and flat. The clever wine-buyer avoids the fading blooms, coming up rosé with the snappiest, most refreshing pinks around.

Even when you know how to spot a decent rosé, it's essential to be aware that many different styles of pink wine are made around the world. A fine, delicate rosé from the cool Loire in France is nothing like a rich, powerful Grenache rosé from South Australia. And dryness/sweetness levels vary, too, so be prepared for that. Then it's essential to choose the right moment to sink some pink; perhaps more so than with any other style of wine, rosé only suits certain occasions.

Summery weather, outside dining, light salads and cold meats, fruit and mild cheeses… all these shout 'rosé!'. I never, ever want pink wine in the deep mid-winter, or with a hearty stew, or when I'm drinking by the fireside. That's probably why we all enjoy rosé on our summer holidays but rarely get a kick out of the bottle we bring home and crack open in chilly October! So, pick a pink with care, and pick the perfect moment to enjoy it.

## TEXTURE

The lightest rosés are thin and lean, even dilute, but the richest are weighty, almost syrupy in richness.

## APPEARANCE

Rosé wine can be anything from almost white, with the very palest tinge of pink, to a bright, sunset peachy-orange, and even a deep cerise, like a light red.

## AROMA

Think of red berries – rosé should always have an appealing,
fresh fragrance of raspberries, cherries, strawberries or
cranberries. Some have more blackcurrant and plums on the
bouquet; others smell of rosehip cordial. Look out for a subtle
hint of grass on leaner styles and even a whiff of vanilla ice
cream – raspberry ripple is quite common!

## FLAVOUR

Those red berries should charge
through on the palate, too, along
with a creaminess on the richer
styles. Some rosés have a thin,
disappointingly short finish,
while the chunkiest have a much
more lingering flavour, like a red
wine, with some slight tannin on
the finish. There should always
be a sense of fresh, crisp acidity
in rosé. Be aware that while
some are bone-dry, others
are medium to sweet.

# FRANCE

FROM DELICATE TO RIPE

French rosé is still pretty popular, from the delicate pinks of the Loire Valley, to the well-balanced, fruity ones of Bordeaux, and the gutsy, rich wines of the south. Roughly speaking, the further south you head, and the warmer the vineyards become, the richer and riper the rosé gets. Across the land, though, the quality of this wine varies a lot, so choose a French rosé very carefully. Pick a good pink and you'll believe France is the master of this style, but choose a dud and you'll never bother again. Which would be a shame.

## LOIRE

Let's start in the Loire Valley in north-central France, where the cool vineyards produce pink wines more delicate, crisp and mouth-watering than those made further south. Unfortunately, this is where you are most likely to come unstuck, as the Loire, a large area with lots of subregions, churns out a wide range of rosé from delicious to dire.

The pale Rosé d'Anjou can be refreshing, if simple in an off-dry style. Made in the area just east of the town of Ancenis, it comes from the rather uninspiring Grolleau grape, which was never destined to make great wine. Rosé d'Anjou is widely available and it is cheap, but there are more exciting pink wines.

Take Cabernet d'Anjou, for example, which is made from a superior grape variety: Cabernet Franc. Like Rosé d'Anjou, it is usually off-dry, but the sweetness is matched by riper, juicier fruitiness, and the quality overall is higher. In the Loire itself, Cabernet d'Anjou is taken more seriously than other rosés. It may be harder to track down, but do try it if you get the chance. Then there's Rosé de Loire, made in Touraine and Anjou-Saumur from Cabernet Franc and sometimes other Loire grapes. This will appeal more to lovers of dry, lip-smacking, thirst-quenching styles of pink.

And finally, the Vins de Pays du Jardin de la France (country wines from the Loire) provide some (usually) decent pink in the form of Cabernet Rosé, which is pleasingly light, dry and tangy, if simple.

## BORDEAUX

Further southwest, in Bordeaux, the rosé (just like the white wine) has improved in recent years and now provides some of the most appealing pink around. The majority of Bordeaux rosés are made from Merlot, so you can expect some of that attractive fruity character so typical of this grape, plus (in the best wines) an attractive aroma and a crisp, succulent finish. A typical flavour is fresh strawberries with a dab of cream. A few wines have a little Cabernet Sauvignon and Cabernet Franc in the mix – here, as anywhere, rosé producers make the most of any red grapes going. Bordeaux rosé is well worth trying. As usual with rosé, make sure to crack open a young wine. Top of any rosé-lover's list is the pink from Château de Sours.

## PROVENCE

In the deeper south of France, Provence is the source of riper, deeply coloured rosés made mainly from Grenache and Cinsault – these wines can have a juicy rosehip and slightly toffeed character. Some arrive in traditional bottles, shaped like a bowling skittle, with a wide-hipped look to them. A fine Provence rosé is delightful and rich enough to stand up to cold meats and even Mediterranean garlic and tomato dishes, but be aware that there are lots of substandard, oxidised wines around.

## REST OF FRANCE

Although plenty of basic table rosé is made in other parts of France, much of it is not exported but simply made to be enjoyed, while young and fresh, in local bars and restaurants.

Pink wines from the Charentes region are a case in point – drunk by the bucketful along the Atlantic coast to wash down moules frites, they are hardly ever seen outside their region. However, another couple of French pinks sometimes encountered overseas are those of Tavel and Lirac in the southern Rhône Valley; these are fairly serious, chunky rosés made from the Rhône red grapes Syrah and Grenache. They taste as though they are packed with ripe red berries, perhaps with a note of spice and caramel. Good stuff. Finally, you may come across Rosé de Riceys, a rare but delicious, still, pink wine made in the Champagne region from the Pinot Noir grape. It has the aroma and flavour of fresh raspberries.

French rosés have their detractors, and I would be the first to agree that quality is alarmingly patchy. But find a decent source of fine French rosé and you'll see why some people love it so much. Many of these discover a favourite local producer while on holiday there, and I'd certainly recommend tasting rosé at the cellar door, as this is where pink wine should be at its most youthful and fresh. Even the simplest, cheapest French rosé can be a delight at such moments. But wherever you are in France, do avoid the ultra-bargain plastic buckets for rosé on sale at the local supermarché as these often taste tired and horrid.

# SPAIN

## TEMPTING, TANGY ROSADO

I reckon more people have been converted to rosé (or rosado, as it is called here) by drinking Spanish versions than any other. There's something about a chilled, tangy glass of rosado, enjoyed with jamón or prawns by the seaside in Spain that makes us go potty for this style of wine. As usual, we tend to bring the wine home and forget to drink it until it is old and faded, so if you enjoy Spanish rosado in situ, make sure you buy fresh, youthful bottles of it at home, too.

## RIOJA AND NAVARRA

Rosado is made in a number of regions from a range of varieties, but the best come from the Rioja and Navarra regions, usually made from either the Tempranillo or Grenache grape (called Garnacha in Spain). Expect the wine to be perfumed and cherryish, dry and mouth-watering – try Chivite's rosado from Navarra for a fine glassful.

## REST OF SPAIN

Once you've tried wines from these well-known winemaking areas, go for a modern rosado from Somontano or a rich one from Priorato to ring the changes. And try the local Spanish Bobal grape which can make moreish rosado in Alicante and Utiel-Requena. Valencia's widely seen, inexpensive rosados are pleasantly fruity and moreish when young.

# OTHER EUROPEAN ROSÉS

## PINK GEMS FROM
## THE OLD WORLD

## PORTUGAL

Portugal became famous (or should that be infamous?) for rosé with the seventies success story Mateus Rosé. The brand still exists, but nowadays the slightly off-dry, spritzy and pale pink isn't as popular as it used to be. Apart from Mateus, there are few other Portuguese rosés, although the odd one, dry and bright, from the Bairrada region makes an appearance.

## ITALY

Italy produces a handful of palatable rosés – or rosatos, as they are known. As in France, the cooler areas, especially the northeast, make crisp, pale, lighter styles, while the warmer south is responsible for richer wines. The fruity, deep-pink Cirò from Calabria, made from the local Gaglioppo grape, is one to sample.

## EASTERN EUROPE

The occasional pink gem pops up from this region, although watch out, as standards are patchy, particularly from Bulgaria. Hungary is a better bet, making some clean crisp and very dry cheapies.

## OTHERS FROM EUROPE

It may surprise you to learn that England makes a handful of decent rosés, from a clutch of different grape varieties. The required crispness and freshness is usually there, owing to our cool climate, although some are distinctly sweeter than others. Greece is another unexpected source of modern rosé, with one or two labels making it on to our shelves in recent years. These are mainly produced from local grape varieties and are rather tasty and ripe.

# USA

## FROM BLUSHING TO GUTSY

There's a type of pink wine made in the US which, strictly speaking, isn't. Pink, that is. It's more a pallid off-white with a faint hint of blush if you hold it up to the light. The aromas are neutral and the flavours are equally disappointing.

## CALIFORNIA

Often sweetish, and distinctly lacking in fruit flavours, these 'blush' wines are popular over there, and to a certain extent, over here, too. They are often made from the Zinfandel grape, another cause for complaint, as 'Zin' can be wonderful when made into a hearty red wine, but is decidedly disappointing when forced into producing these weak, bland semi-rosés. 'White Zinfandel', blush

Zinfandel and other lookalikes are widely available on the export market, and, for some people, the sweetness and blandness will be a plus, but do be aware that there are much more exciting rosé wines out there!

Even from California. You see, some of the better West Coast winemakers have now decided to make much riper, deeply coloured rosés, and these wines (in my view, anyway) knock those pale blush rosés for six. Sometimes made from Syrah, occasionally from Grenache, they are pretty gutsy and rich. Try Fetzer's Syrah Rosé as a prime example of new-wave Californian pink wine or one from Bonny Doon's range.

# AUSTRALIA

## RICH, VIBRANT AND STRONG

Anyone who hates pale and uninteresting rosé should take note – the Aussies make wonderfully rich, vibrant, alcoholic, no-nonsense rosé that is certainly not for wimps!

## SOUTH AUSTRALIA

OK, so there aren't exactly hundreds of examples around, but a wine such as Charles Melton's Rosé of Virginia, a cerise-coloured, weighty mouthful of strawberry and cranberry, with a creamy finish, proves the point very well. This wine is made from Grenache in the warm Barossa Valley in South Australia. Geoff Merrill, also working in South Australia, makes another strong, robust rosé.

## OTHER REGIONS

You'll find a (very) few rosés in most of the other wine-producing areas of Australia, but look out for the slightly crisper style emerging from cooler spots like the Yarra Vally in Victoria and Tasmania. Hardly any of these make it on to the export market though.

The big, buxom style of Aussie rosé will age for longer than weedier pinks – a good year or so in the case of Melton's wine. The best time to bring out these bottles (and this goes for other very ripe New World styles of pink too) is at a barbie, when they make a great match for prawns, salmon steaks and grilled vegetable kebabs.

# ROSÉS FROM THE REST OF THE WORLD

## WORTHWHILE PINK GEMS

### CHILE AND ARGENTINA

These countries are not well-known for rosé, but a few tasty examples come out of both. Chile produces mainly Merlot- or Cabernet Sauvignon-based rosés, usually fresh and aromatic, while some wineries around the Argentinian winemaking capital of Mendoza turn out sprightly, fruity Syrah-based pinks. South American rosé can be good value for money. Try Miguel Torres' inexpensive example from Chile in the first instance.

### REST OF THE WORLD

New Zealand makes one or two worthwhile rosés, particularly in the Marlborough region of the South Island, where the wines taste light, lean and a little grassy. Merlot is usually used. Another part of the world more important for rosé, although perhaps less well-known, is North Africa. Several North African countries produce them from the Southern French grapes Grenache, Syrah and Cinsault. Morocco is the best source: the wines can be more than palatable.

# MATCHING ROSÉ WITH FOOD

DECENT ROSÉ IS DELECTABLE ON ITS OWN: TRULY REFRESHING, MOUTH-TINGLING, VIBRANTLY FRUITY WINE FOR A HOT SUMMER'S DAY. It also partners food well, but choose carefully as very rich food will overpower its delicate flavours. A mild goat's cheese salad, a plate of cold ham (jamón), fresh seafood (especially prawns) and pasta with a creamy sauce all make great matches. Very cold, off-dry pink is fairly good at washing down lightly spicy dishes – vegetable samosas spring to mind.

# STORING AND SERVING

ROSÉ SHOULD BE CONSUMED WHILE IT IS FRESH AND YOUNG, AS IT SOON LOSES ITS INVITING AROMA AND FLAVOUR. Make sure to buy the youngest vintage you can find and never get palmed off with an elderly bottle of rosé. There's no point in cellaring rosé – drink it up soon after purchase and, once opened, keep it in the fridge and finish it within a day or two. The exceptions are the heartiest, blockbuster Aussie rosés, which may last up to a year.

# FIRST TASTE

■ Be aware that ROSÉ IS A FRAGILE WINE and loses its fruity flavours sooner than most. Always buy and drink it up soon after bottling – and once opened, don't leave rosé hanging around. Either finish it within twenty-four hours or ditch it!

■ Pick your moment to crack open a bottle as ROSÉ SUITS HOT-WEATHER DRINKING, either with no food at all, or with light snacks and salads. This is not a wine to drink with rich, hearty dishes.

■ ALWAYS SERVE ROSÉ WELL-CHILLED – even colder than you might serve rich white wines, as the chill emphasises the refreshing, tangy nature of the wine. Frosty glasses of icy rosé always look appealing.

■ If you ever get the chance, ENJOY ROSÉ WHEN TRAVELLING in the wine region itself – it will taste all the more lively and vibrantly fruity for being young and fresh.

# BUYER'S GUIDE

■ Although Rosé d'Anjou from the Loire Valley, France, is one of the most commonly seen rosés, it is not always the best – TRY OTHER FRENCH PINKS, especially Bordeaux rosé, and, if you see it, rosé from Tavel or Lirac in the Rhône Valley.

■ They are usually a little more expensive than European ones, but AUSTRALIAN ROSÉS ARE RICHER AND HEARTIER, and the top ones are serious bottles that would go down well at a barbie.

■ Always, always, BUY THE YOUNGEST ROSÉ YOU CAN FIND either in the shops or off a wine list. Aim for a very recent vintage. Reject anything too old or your pink will have lost its bloom.

■ Taste even the very cheapest rosés if you get the chance because THERE ARE A FEW GENUINE BARGAINS out there. It's well worth sampling a few different labels of inexpensive rosé at the start of summer and picking the one you like best for future buying.

# MOVING ON

■ FOR PARTY PINKS, TRY CHILEAN OR ARGENTINIAN ROSÉS. There aren't too many around, but they are good value and make a change from French or Spanish ones.

■ Move on from boring basic Californian 'blush' and TRADE UP TO THE NEW-WAVE, GUTSY WEST COAST ROSÉS with bags more colour and flavour.

■ TRY MOROCCAN ROSÉ, which is surprisingly tasty from a country not exactly renowned for its winemaking prowess!

■ EXPERIMENT BY MATCHING ROSÉS WITH A WIDE RANGE OF DISHES, such as mildly spicy food, cold meats, barbecues, buffet fare – you'll be surprised at how many exciting partners you find.

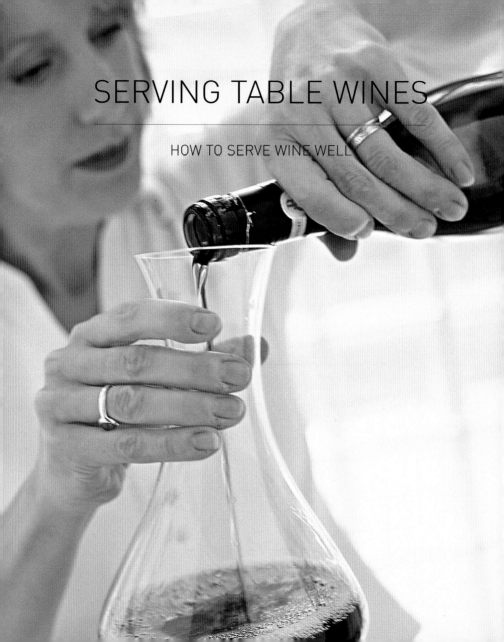

# SERVING TABLE WINES

## HOW TO SERVE WINE WELL

Is it just me, or are certain bottles of wine sometimes very difficult to get into? Natural corks seem to get stuck with annoying frequency and I have to call on a strong man (okay, my husband) to get them out. Plastic stoppers, which are sometimes made to look just like bark corks, are easier in this respect, but tend to be difficult to pull off the corkscrew! Perhaps these are two further reasons why the screwcap is making such a comeback – it's not just about combating cork taint. However, the following tips should help you get into any bottle, whether it has a natural or a plastic cork.

Buy a not-very-expensive, simple, lever-type corkscrew called a 'waiter's friend'. (Waiters keep them in their pockets.) Once mastered, it's hard to beat a waiter's friend, even with a fancy designer corkscrew. Screw it in, then use the ledge on the side of the handle to push against the bottle as you slowly and steadily lever the cork out. This is not so good with modern bottles that have flattened, wide rims (flange tops); indeed, these are the most difficult wines to open without chipping the glass neck, so if opening ain't your strong point, steer clear of the flange design fad.

Here's how to serve wine well. Remove any bits of cork crumble around the lip of the bottle, simply because they will look bad in a glass (they don't affect the flavour). Then slowly pour the wine into the glass, filling it only about one-third of the way up. This doesn't mean you are stingy, but it lets you swirl the liquid around, and savour its appearance and aroma. Do what the experts do – fill it up frequently, but never right to the top (unless it's a Champagne flute, which looks odd half-empty). This is helpful for keeping whites cold, too, as it means the wine can stay in the bottle in a cool spot, rather than sitting around warming up in your glass.

Pour rich reds, especially older ones, with great care. They may have a sediment that has collected in the bottom of the bottle over the years (or along its side if it has been in a rack). No one wants to sip a mouthful of black gunk, so remove the sediment by decanting the bottle gradually and cautiously into a glass decanter (or a clean jug), and stop as soon as you see the sediment start to appear in the liquid. Chuck away the dregs.

It's also worth decanting rich, tannic reds which don't have a sediment, as exposure to the air mellows them and helps allow their aroma and flavour to emerge. Forget about messing around opening the bottle half an hour before dinner; it won't have a great effect on the liquid. Instead, decant the wine into another container, (see page 140), or even pour it into big-bowled glasses and swoosh it around firmly to aerate at the table.

The ideal wineglass is neither a pricey, multi-faceted crystal one nor a modern, brightly coloured one. To see your wine properly, go for plain glass, and choose a thin one, as that feels much nicer on the mouth than chunky, thick glass does and is more elegant all round. Pick glasses with long stems, so you can hold the glass there, rather than wrapping your fingers round the bowl and warming up the wine. And go for a fairly big bowl so you can swirl the wine effectively and release its aroma. Serve sherry and port from ordinary white-wine glasses – throw those old-fashioned little schooners away!

# WINE ACCESSORIES

THE PASSIONATE WINE BUFF MIGHT WISH TO OWN A WHOLE HOST OF WINE ACCESSORIES; FANCY PIECES OF KIT THAT SHOULD BE THERE TO HELP WITH THE PROCESS OF SERVING AND ENJOYING WINE, BUT WHICH ARE PROBABLY THERE ONLY TO IMPRESS! From the drip-stop silver collar, to the wine thermometer, to the pewter coaster, these collectables are only useful to a degree and, if truth be told, you can get by fine without recourse to any of them. One of the most useful, in my view, is the humble, inexpensive chiller sleeve, a frozen plastic 'arm-band' which chills wine adequately well in a matter of minutes. As I have explained opposite, a decanter is a good idea, but to be honest, a good glass jug will suffice. Own these two items, plus a good corkscrew (the cheap waiter's friend, lever-style model is fine), and you don't really need anything else. Except a decent wine, of course!

# DETECTING FAULTS IN WINE

It doesn't pay to be a wimp if you think your wine is faulty. Many of us are embarrassed about complaining, when we are quite comfortable to make a fuss about poor food, bad clothes or rip-off holidays. I'll let you in on a secret that some of the wine trade want to keep hidden: there's no special mystery about faulty wine.

If you don't like a wine, take it back to the shop, or send it back if you're in a restaurant. You do not have to understand the problem like a top-ranking merchant does. Just explain that the wine tastes of vinegar, or smells musty, or looks cloudy or so on. As long as you haven't drained the bottle (that would be taking the mick) you can expect to receive a replacement – a new bottle of the same wine or a similarly priced one.

There is one proviso when returning wine, however: try not to complain that the wine is not the style you like. There's a big difference between a faulty wine and one that doesn't suit you. A kind retailer might replace a wine bought in error, but not everyone will. Restaurants are especially snooty about this.

If you keep buying the wrong sort of wine, make sure you ask more questions about a bottle before you buy it, or read this book carefully before you go shopping. You can't expect to take back an extremely cheap white, say, just because it is a bit boring, or a bargain-basement red because it is a touch over-oaky. No, we're talking faults here: nasty, bitter, acidic, over-sweet, mouldy, flabby, oxidised wine. No one should shell out good money for something that tastes truly revolting!

The most prevalent wine fault is caused by cork taint. Corked wine has nothing to do with a crumbling cork. It means a mould-affected cork has spoilt the wine, giving a musty aroma and cardboard flavour (think damp cardboard, old kitchen clothes, even mushrooms). This trait can be quite pronounced in some wines, but disarmingly subtle in others, sometimes just deadening the fresh-fruit aroma and taste of the wine. Corked wine gets worse the longer it is opened, so if you're not sure, wait awhile and try it again. If you suspect the wine is corked (you can't prove it and shouldn't have to), take or send it back, and demand a replacement. Despite some efforts on the part of the cork industry, the number of corked bottles remains unacceptably high – some estimates put it as one in eight bottles. This is the main reason why plastic corks and screwcaps are sometimes used instead. Use of screwcaps for premium wines, especially in New Zealand and Australia, is on the rise.

Other faults to look out for include oxidised wine (where air has got in and spoilt it), wine with 'foreign objects' in it (I found tiny fruit flies on one memorable occasion), and heavily sulphured wine. Sulphur is used as a preservative when most wines are bottled, but overuse leads to a wine which smells of struck matches, and this may cause problems to asthma sufferers and others allergic to this chemical. The stricter regulations for organic wine mean it usually contains less sulphur. Send stinking sulphurous wines back!

Don't worry about wine that has thrown a natural sediment (see page 142) or ones with little white crystals in the bottle. The latter are harmless tartrate deposits which won't affect the taste of your wine.

# STORING WINE

## YOU DON'T NEED A SERIOUS STORAGE PLAN

The vast majority of the bottles we buy are cracked open and enjoyed within twenty-four days of purchase – despite all you hear about cellaring or 'laying down' wine, few of us actually do it. There's nothing wrong with this 'drink 'em quick' attitude. Many reds produced today are deliberately created in an easy-going, soft and smooth style which makes for delicious early enjoyment. And a high number of fairly simple, light, dry whites, rosés and sparklers should be opened while young or they lose their fresh appeal. But most of us have the odd bottle lying around – something a bit special, perhaps, or a wine that we are saving for a particular occasion. You don't need a serious storage plan to keep a few bottles for a week or two, obviously, but do think about where and how you store them if they are hanging around for more than a few days. Above all, keep your wine in a cool, dark spot – this fragile liquid suffers if it is put in a hot place (or, worse, where temperatures fluctuate a lot), or if it is kept in direct sunlight. I'm especially bothered by the latest trend for mini wine racks placed near the oven – often a feature of the modern fitted kitchen. The kitchen is not an ideal room for wine at all as it gets much too hot in there, nearly every day. Wine stored in warm, sunny places quickly loses its fresh fruitiness, so don't leave it on the windowsill in high summer, either!

## MAKESHIFT CELLARS

Instead, buy a multi-millionaire's house with a big cellar, fitted with state-of-the-art wine racks. Only kidding. There are plenty of places in the ordinary home where wine can be kept safely and sensibly. The cupboard under the stairs is usually a good bet – make sure you don't store any white spirits or pungent paints down there as well, since there's some evidence that wine can be affected by strong-smelling substances. Lay bottles on their sides if you're keeping them for more than a couple of weeks. This stops the cork from drying out – a shrivelled-up cork can let air in to the bottle and spoil the wine. If you invest in a small wine rack, go for a wooden one as metal racks can easily tear the labels when the bottles are removed. Alternative spots for storing a few bottles include: the bottom of a wardrobe, a downstairs cloakroom, under the spare bed… anywhere, really, where it stays relatively cool and dark and where you are not likely to disturb your bottles and break them. The garage is not a great idea, as it can get very cold, and often has petrol and paint fumes. Some people worry about leaving white and sparkling wine in the fridge for any length of time. There's nothing wrong with storing an everyday bottle in there for a day or two, but watch out it isn't too cold when you serve it, as a serious chill can mute the flavour and aroma.

## PROFESSIONAL WINE STORAGE

What if you are developing a real passion for wine and want to start a serious collection? A cellar is the best storage option; it tends to be cooler, darker and sometimes a little humid: perfect conditions for wine. If you are lucky enough to have a cellar, empty it of all smelly substances, but don't repaint it or wash it down with lots of cleaning fluid – wine doesn't mind dirt but it may be affected by chemicals in the air. Line a wall or two with decent racks and buy some cellar tags for putting over the necks of your bottles to help you identify them. It's possible to keep wine in its original case, as well as on a rack; as long as the bottles are lying on their sides and can't break, they will be fine. It may be worth keeping a 'cellar book' to record when you opened the wine and what it tasted like – especially if you have lots of the same bottles stored there, as you can chart that wine's development.

## OTHER STORAGE OPTIONS

Of course there are wine buffs who lack cellars, but have built up an impressive collection nonetheless. One option is a temperature-controlled unit that looks just like a fridge, but is filled with racks and designed to keep fine wine in exactly the right conditions. These are expensive (expect to splash out at least £800) but cheaper than moving of course, and may be worth the investment if you are embarking on a lifetime of fine-wine collecting. Even more pricey are spiral-shaped cellars that are bored into the ground floor of your home (the door is hidden under a rug in the living room or kitchen, for example). These cost nearer £5,000– £10,000 but are impressive: a small circular underground cellar is created, lined with wine racks and with a central staircase to provide access. One of these may add some value onto your home. Flat owners need not apply…

Most of us find some solution to the problem. We don't have a cellar in our country cottage but we do have a reasonable collection of fine wine, which lives in a cool, walk-in cupboard which the previous owner used as a 'gun' room. I know a wine-crazy Londoner who keeps his loot in the outside loo at the bottom of his garden, with a thermostat to control the temperature. Others keep theirs with a wine storage specialist.

## WINES WORTH HANGING ON TO

As mentioned above, most ordinary, inexpensive wine is meant to be consumed soon after you buy it. That goes for soft, light, 'everyday' reds as well as dry whites. As a rule of thumb, the lighter and less substantial the wine (think Pinot Grigio, Muscadet, basic Beaujolais, cheap fizz), the more quickly you must open it. Richer 'everyday' wines (non-European Chardonnay, Cab-Shiraz blends, ordinary Rhône reds) last a bit longer unopened – up to a year after purchase, before starting to lose their vibrant flavours and aromas. Note that red Rioja, even a very expensive label, is aged at the winery in Spain and released ready to drink. Likewise LBV (late-bottled vintage) and tawny ports. Don't be tempted to store them for long.

But some wines are supposed to be kept – they actually taste better if you lay them down for a period. Among these are young, tough premium reds from Bordeaux (claret); vintage Champagnes; fine German Rieslings, both sweet and dry (and similar bottles from Austria); rich, tannic Cabernets and Cabernet blends from the southern hemisphere; top Australian Semillons; top-of-the-range Rhône reds; Barbarescos, Amarones and Barolos from Italy; and best Loire Valley whites. These wines will all benefit from some bottle-age (assuming you buy recent vintages), becoming more mellow, their acidity softer, their flavours more well-knit, with honeyed undertones in the whites and smoother, earthier, even gamey notes in the reds.

It's obviously a matter of taste whether you like mature wines or youthful ones. In the case of certain styles, like red burgundy, there is something to be said for the bright, red-fruit character of the younger wines and the truffley, horsey, richly gamey character of older ones. Both are valid. In the UK, fine wines were traditionally drunk when they were very mature (the French were often shocked by this and rather sniffily called it *le goût Anglais*, 'the English taste'.) Now younger wines are preferred with more fresh-fruit flavours. As with so many things in the world of wine, work out which suits you best. A serious collection should give you ample opportunity to try out wines both young and old!

# HOW TO TASTE WINE

DON'T SKIP THIS IF YOU ASSUME TASTING WINE LIKE A PRO MEANS LOOKING LIKE AN IDIOT! Okay, it might do, but taking your time to think about this precious liquid will definitely help you learn an enormous amount about it. I reckon ninety-nine per cent of all wine slips down our throat without touching the sides, so that while a little of its unique character comes through, not much does. If you look at wine carefully, then smell it properly, and finally take your time tasting it, you should notice a lot of interesting characteristics starting to emerge, for good or bad. Then you will almost certainly enjoy fine wine a great deal more. The best thing about tasting is that no one is 'right' or 'wrong' in deciding what a wine tastes like. It's just a matter of building up points of reference that mean something to the individual taster. If you still think you'll look like an idiot, practise the following steps in the bath, spitting out at your toes – that's what a lot of the experts do – until it feels like second nature!

# LOOK

The appearance of any wine can tell you much about the sort of style to expect.

## SNIFF

Swirl the liquid to release its aroma –
it's an important part of a wine's appeal.

## SLURP

Swoosh the wine around your mouth
to bring out the full flavour. Think
about its taste and texture.

## SPIT

The 'finish' of a wine is important.
Consider its richness or lightness,
length of flavour and general appeal.

## LOOK

The appearance of wine is important, so really peer at the liquid in your wine glass. It helps if you choose a plain glass, not a cut or coloured one, with a tall stem. Tipping the glass to one side helps, holding it way down the stem, especially when assessing the depth of colour in your red: look at the rim of the liquid, not the middle. A wine should look clear, not cloudy, without bits of sediment floating in it (see page 142). Look at the viscosity of the liquid: a rich, thick wine leaves noticeable trails, or 'legs', down the side of the glass after you have swirled. This can indicate high alcohol levels or sweetness. Red wines with an almost bluish tinge tend to taste younger than those with a brick-red, brownish colour, and those that have turned brown may well be past it. In whites, a deep golden colour indicates a rich wine, which could be oaky or lusciously sweet. A pale-straw hue means a drier, lighter style in your glass.

## SNIFF

Now for the aroma. ('Bouquet' is another, somewhat old-fashioned term for describing the aroma; some experts call it the 'nose'.) Swirl the wine around your glass before you smell it, as this releases its aroma. Now stick your nose near the liquid and take a big sniff, or a series of small sniffs. A wine's scent is very important, acting as an introduction to the flavour. This simple test is often overlooked, so linger over it. Does the wine smell appealing or not? Does it seem clean and fresh or sulphurous, vegetal or musty? Is it a subtle smell or a rich, pungent one? Think about the fruit character – citrus fruits, perhaps, or red berries, or bananas. Maybe take it further: what sort of citrus fruits (lemons, oranges, grapefruit...), what sort of berries (raspberries, redcurrants...), fresh bananas or banana sweeties, or even banoffee pie? Look out for vanilla, cream, spice and pepper, too, and other more eclectic nuances.

## SLURP

Take a small sip and swirl the liquid around your mouth, even drawing some air through it and swooshing it around to release the full flavour. Look for similar characteristics in the flavour – fruit, cream, spice – but at the same time consider other elements, such as its weight, structure or body and how acidic or refreshing it is. Try to decide whether this is a rich or a light wine, a tart wine, or a heavy, dense or oily one. Is it tannic – tannins produce a furry sensation in the mouth, like sucking on a tea bag – or bone-dry or honeyed and sweet? Think about whether it is simply a big, rich, impressive wine, perhaps one that you might not want to drink in any quantity, but which is simply a show-off in character! Lighter, simpler wines are sometimes more enjoyable or food-friendly. Finally, is the wine well-balanced, or does it have over-the-top tannins, mouth-puckering acidity or is its sweetness out of kilter?

## SPIT

Professional wine tasters (almost) always spit wine out to save their sobriety, but they don't stop assessing the wine as they spit. The 'finish' of a wine is the final important factor. Does it leave a lingering flavour or does it disappear from the taste buds in a disappointing way? This provides another opportunity to assess texture: is it a rich, gloopy wine or a thin, light one? Again, look out for those unusual nuances – perhaps black pepper in a Syrah, or chocolate in a Merlot – as these often come through on the finish more than ever. Sometimes wine faults show up on the finish. A corked wine might leave a musty taste in the mouth, while an over-acidic wine may be wincingly tart at the very end. Tannins also tend to show through at this stage more than any other. If your wine leaves a chewy, furry, 'tea-leaf' texture in your mouth, it's tannic and may need time to soften up, or a rare steak to accompany it.